Thomas Merton
a mind awake in the dark

THOMAS MERTON
a mind awake in the dark

Papers

presented at
THE THIRD
GENERAL CONFERENCE
of the THOMAS MERTON SOCIETY
of GREAT BRITAIN AND IRELAND
at OAKHAM SCHOOL,
MARCH 2000

Edited by
PAUL M. PEARSON
DANNY SULLIVAN
IAN THOMSON

P³P

Published in Great Britain 2002
THREE PEAKS PRESS
9 Croesonen Road
Abergavenny,
Monmouthshire NP7 6AE
mail@p3p.org   http://p3p.org

Designed & set in Joanna at Three Peaks Press

With thanks to Elizabeth Skelton

Printed in Wales at Gwasg Dinefwr, Llandybie

A CIP record for this publication
is available from the British Library

ISBN   1–902093–06–2

Contents

"...I am glad to be able to tell someone at Oakham that I really bear the school a deep affection, with sentiments of gratitude that will not die... I never regret having gone to Oakham. On the contrary, I am very glad that I was sent there rather than to some larger school, for Oakham had something of simplicity and sincerity about it that one might look for in vain elsewhere."

THOMAS MERTON *to* C.J. DIXON,
November 9th, 1954

INTRODUCTION

THE THIRD GENERAL MEETING OF THE THOMAS MERTON SOCIETY OF GREAT Britain and Ireland, the first of the new millennium, focused on Merton's essay *Day of a Stranger* both in the title of the meeting and in some of the keynote sessions. As so much energy across the globe centered on celebrating the dawn of the third millennium, Merton's words written in his hermitage in the Kentucky woods struck a clear note, sounding like a solitary bell echoing through the night.

Day of a Stranger was written by Merton in May 1965 in answer to a request from a Latin American editor who asked him for a description of a "typical day" in Merton's life. This typical day was different from that experienced by the majority of monks at the Abbey of Gethsemani, let alone by the majority of other people outside the monastery walls. As Merton's perception of himself had changed through the course of his monastic life – from having turned his back on the world in *The Seven Storey Mountain* to that of an "innocent bystander" in the late fifties and ultimately to a "guilty bystander"– so his contemplation gave him insights into both his relationship to the world and his strangeness, his strangerness, to it.

Merton's day, beginning at "two-fifteen in the morning, when the night is darkest and most silent" gave him the contemplative distance as "a mind awake in the dark" to look into that darkness and to face it. In this essay he refers to the darkness of the American South, Selma, Birmingham and Mississippi; the darkness of the atomic cloud brought home to him daily by the strategic air command bombers flying overheard, and the noise of the guns of Fort Knox which he could hear in his hermitage in the Gethsemani woods; the darkness of the growing conflict in Vietnam; and even the darkness of the monastic life "hot with words like 'must,' 'ought' and 'should.'" In the darkness of night, Merton discovered God's mercy and the love necessary to embrace his sisters and brothers.

The third general meeting of the Thomas Merton Society of Great Britain and Ireland once again brought together a diverse group of people from all over the British Isles and much further afield. One particular blessing of the meeting was the presence of a group of hermits from Holy Hill Hermitage in Ireland. The gift of music they brought echoed through the conference from the sung grace at the opening dinner to the final strains of 'My soul is like the sparrow,' a favorite spiritual of Martin Luther King, at the closing liturgy.

Alongside music, poetry was once again an important part of the conference, with the opening session featuring a panel presentation on a selection of Merton's poetry representing the major periods in his poetic output, and we are grateful to New Directions for permission to publish the poems used at that session in this book. Some of the poems from the opening session were featured, in the evening, in the first British performance of a selection of songs from the Niles-Merton Song Cycle performed by Damian O'Keeffe and accompanied by Ivan Linford.

The papers in this book explore many of the themes of *Day of a Stranger* and present some of the many ways in which Merton is still "a mind awake in the dark" for us at the beginning of this new millennium, almost forty years since his essay was written. Through his example may we all be found awake when the Lord of all ages comes.

PAUL M. PEARSON

Acknowledgement

Merton's poems in the section entitled 'The Poetry of Thomas Merton' (pp. 61ff.) are the copyright of the Merton Legacy Trust, © 1963, 1968 & 1977 by the Trustees of the Merton Legacy Trust. The poems are used by permission of New Directions Publishing Corporation and the Trustees of the Merton Legacy Trust.

PRESIDENTIAL ADDRESS
Merton and Traherne:
The Two Thomases

CANON A.M. 'DONALD' ALLCHIN

IN THINKING OF WHAT I WOULD SAY THIS EVENING I HAD A DILEMMA. I wondered whether to speak in very general terms, Merton and the new millennium; or Merton and the spiritual and theological situation of our Post-Modernist age; or perhaps a little more particularly Merton in relationship, I believe a potentially very fruitful relationship, to the current of theological and spiritual writing which is emerging here in Britain, a current which is sometimes described in terms of *generous orthodoxy*. That is a current which as far as Anglicans are concerned can be represented above all by the work of two outstanding theologians, one an Irish layman from Dublin, and the other a Welsh archbishop from Swansea; David Ford, Regius Professor at Cambridge and Dr Rowan Williams, Archbishop of Wales, one of our keynote speakers in our conference two years ago. It is perhaps particularly good for the English amongst us to recognise that Anglican and English are not necessarily synonymous!

But the more I thought about it the more I decided to avoid generalities, we have had too many of them in the turn of the millennium; and instead to concentrate on a few minute particulars, and in particular on one quite narrow topic, Merton's attitude to and indebtedness to some of the classical Anglican writers of the seventeenth century.

No-one could pretend that these classical writers bulk large in Merton's work. Of course he had had some knowledge of the poets of the period from his student days at Columbia when, not unexpectedly, he had been particularly drawn to John Donne and Richard Crashaw. Later one can find expressions of particular interest in Henry Vaughan. Indeed Merton was interested not only in Vaughan's poetry but also in his prose writing, for instance in his translation of the fifth century Latin writer Eucherius. Merton even thought at one time of trying to make an edition of Vaughan's translation of his work on the solitary life.

But in a letter of 1964, Merton writes of this classical period of Anglican writing with a kind of uneasiness, almost a wistful nostalgia. "It seems to me that the best of Anglicanism is unexcelled..." But then of course we have to recognise that it doesn't always reach its best.

> For my part I will try to cling to the best and be as English a Catholic as one in my position can be. I do think it terribly important for Roman Catholics now plunging into the vernacular, to have some sense of the Anglican tradition.

But Merton goes on to say that he is not at all sure how far that can happen in practice. The language, the style and the ethos of the seventeenth century is, as he says, "perhaps no longer within reach of the majority in this country now and is perhaps no longer relevant."[1]

But if we look carefully we begin to see that there are a few passages in the Journals which show how much these seventeenth century writers could mean to him. We discover, for instance, that he had the *Preces Privatae of* Lancelot Andrewes in the hermitage at Gethsemani, and that he had recourse to them in moments of darkness and desolation. It is after all Andrewes who is the greatest of these post-Reformation Anglican writers, and it is he, more than anyone else, who, through the illumination of his sermons and his prayers, gave inspiration to some of the outstanding Anglican poets of the seventeenth century. Not only the seventeenth century writers drew their inspiration from him; it was to Andrewes that one of the greatest Anglo-American poets of the twentieth century, T.S.Eliot, turned in the moment of his definitive affirmation of the Catholic faith of the Church.

So it is not only interesting, but moving, to read Merton's Journal entry for December 3,1964, beginning with a quotation from the *Preces Privatae*

> Evening; the heart is deceitful above all things, the heart is deep and full of windings, the old man is covered up in a thousand wrappings.[2]

Merton comments,

> True sad words. I would not have felt the truth of them so much if I had not had so much solitude these days with rain coming down on the roof and hiding the valley. Rain in the night, the nuisance of water in the buckets. Cutting wood behind the house, a faint smell of hickory

smoke from the chimney, while I taste and see that I am deceitful and that most of my troubles are rooted in my own bitterness. Is this what solitude is for? Then it is good, but I must pray for the strength to bear it! (the heart is deceitful and does not want this—but God is greater than my heart!)

And then again come lines of Lancelot Andrewes,

I will acknowledge my faults O Lord, O who will give scourges to my mind, that they spare not my sins?[3]

Perhaps even more striking is the entry for a few days later.

In the hermitage one must pray or go to seed. The pretence of prayer will not suffice. Just sitting will not suffice. It has to be real—yet what can one do? Solitude puts you with your back to the wall (or your face to it!) and this is good. One prays to pray. Donne's poems and Lancelot Andrewes.

Having seen how Andrewes could be of help to Merton at times of darkness and testing, it is interesting to see him coming to the rescue again at times of thanksgiving and fulfilment.

Exactly three years later in December 1967, at the end of the first retreat for contemplative nuns at Gethsemani, which brought Merton such unexpected joy and encouragement, he notes of the concluding mass, "I opened with a prayer of Lancelot Andrewes instead of the Confiteor," and at the end of the mass he turned to Lancelot Andrewes again, presumably making use of his version of the postcommunion prayer from the liturgy of St Basil, and also a prayer from the old Syrian liturgy for hermits. "Then we sat and had coffee and had a wonderful time. The hermitage is blessed with the memory of it."[4]

Among the seventeenth century writers however, perhaps the one whom Merton appreciated most was Thomas Traherne. Merton wrote very little about him; there is a page or two of luminous analysis in Mystics And Zen Masters when, significantly, he compares him with Julian of Norwich. He can hardly give him greater commendation than that! There is also a reference to him in one of the best of his letters to his Aunt Kit in New Zealand. In May 1964, in a long chatty letter, he remarks

Lately I have been reading about hermits and recluses in early Celtic Christianity and in England. Wales was a very monastic and eremitical sort of place. I think we all have some of this in our blood.

And then he veers off

Did you ever read Thomas Traherne? He is one of the very best and most delightful of Anglican writers.[5]

With this reference to Thomas Traherne I come to the point where I should perhaps have begun this address. For I had at first thought of speaking entirely about Traherne and Merton. I am very glad that we shall have at least one presentation on that subject during this conference. I thought of doing this, first because I felt sure that there is a deep, if hitherto largely unrecognised, affinity between Merton and Traherne, but secondly because I wanted to say at least something about the recent discovery of major, unpublished and hitherto unknown Traherne manuscripts.

This discovery has added another chapter to the almost unbelievable story of the long series of discoveries of Traherne manuscripts which has gone on all through the twentieth century and which reached a climax three years ago with the finding of a new long poem in the Folger Shakespeare Library in Washington, and a big composite manuscript in the Lambeth Palace Library in London. It is as if Traherne himself, or his guardian angel, or the divine providence at work through what looks like chance, had kept hidden for more than three centuries, writings which now confront us with a major mystical theologian, a startling and original thinker, in the England of the Restoration monarchy.

When Traherne died in 1674 only one of his books had been published. Another one was in process of publication and it appeared soon after his death. But neither book made much, if any, impression on his contemporaries or their successors. It was only at the beginning of the twentieth century when the first two major manuscripts were discovered and published, The Poems and the Centuries of Meditations, that Traherne began to be recognised as at least a significant devotional writer of his time. He is a man who can convey to us in wonderful poetic prose, a childhood vision of a transfigured, unfallen world, the world of Eden. That is the impression of Traherne which by and large has remained with the general public down to today. There are a number of fine poems, and there are a number of wonderful pieces of prose which have found their way into many anthologies. In them Traherne speaks of this world as a world in which the glory of eternity is seen shining out through all the things of time.

But throughout the last fifty or sixty years, other manuscripts of Traherne have kept turning up. The most remarkable of these was the one found three years ago in Lambeth Palace Library. This work has as yet not been published, and the scholar who was working on its transcription, a brilliant and delightful teacher at Trinity College in Cambridge, Jeremy Maule, died quite suddenly and unexpectedly, of cancer, a little over a year ago. So the publication of the manuscript is delayed. But what is already becoming clear from the five different pieces contained in it is something which had already been becoming evident through the earlier discoveries of Traherne's works. That is to say that Traherne is not only a beautiful spiritual writer but also a coherent theological thinker, and, what is more, a more powerful and creative figure than has previously been recognised.

Traherne will not fit into our usual way of seeing things. He insists that we begin to fit into his way of seeing things. Something of this quality of Traherne the theologian is conveyed in the last chapter of David Ford's recent book *Self And Salvation*; where David Ford, who knew Jeremy Maule personally, writes of Traherne with remarkable insight.

David Ford points out that Traherne was writing in a time of great political, social and religious turmoil, "having to rethink his faith and practice after the Reformation, the Counter Reformation, Galileo and Cromwell and the founding of the Royal Society..."

In this context it was easy for theologians to become defensive and merely reactionary. Traherne was determined not to do this. He was convinced of the need to maintain the tradition which he had received,

> but he does not go about it defensively. Instead he meets the new enlarged horizons with an even larger one—a fresh conception of the infinity of God in interaction with creation, in which the new scientific discoveries play a part. He responds to confidence in human thought and pride in human freedom, not by detracting from humanity but by stretching his thinking in order to do justice to God as well as to all that is known about the world, and by revelling in the risk God takes in allowing the completion of creation to rely on human freedom.

Traherne is impatient with divines and schoolmen "who have interpreted the image of God in humanity far too constrictedly, leaving out the most wonderful aspects of God." [6]

Speaking a few days ago on the telephone, to one of the scholars who is continuing Jeremy Maule's work on this manuscript, I was amused and intrigued to find her saying, "the more one studies these late manuscripts the more it becomes clear what an enormous amount of writing Traherne did in the last four or five years of his life. It is almost unbelievable." I could only laugh to hear in her puzzlement the identical puzzlement which many who have studied Merton have felt at the enormous creativity of the last decade of his life, the nondisintegrating explosion of interest, concern, thought, attention and love which marks the years of his maturity at the monastery and in the hermitage. How did he find time for it all?

Some people, after they die, seem to go further away from us and to become diminished by the passage of time. In others precisely the reverse seems to happen. Merton does not grow further away, he comes closer to us, perhaps as we begin to catch up with him in some respects. His nearness to us does not diminish, more and more people find him speaking directly to them. The "mind awake in the dark" is present and active in the darkness of our new millennium, present in the darkness of our own searching, of our own awareness of our lostness and our failures. As a reading of The Intimate Merton makes clear in a new way, even to those who may think they know Merton's work well, there is in that writing of his and in his whole life, an extraordinary capacity for communication, which shares itself, gives itself to us utterly.

I know few better descriptions of this quality than that which is to be found in an essay of Elizabeth Jennings who is herself a poet who knows what she is talking of when she tells us of the things of God. This passage however comes not from an essay on Merton but from an essay on Traherne; you must judge how far we could apply it to Merton.

> The poetic prose of his meditations is an example of the art of sharing, of participation. It is an art wholly accessible, in no way private... he wears no masks, casts no concealing shadow. He is in the deepest sense a man possessed. What possesses him is a sense of God and this he wishes to share, distribute. He gives himself away to us in such a way that his work becomes our property. Part of our life.

So Elizabeth Jennings writing about Traherne almost forty years ago.[7]

How much the meaning of her words is multiplied and deepened now that we know so much more of the scope of Traherne's vision than was known then. How they are multiplied again and deepened beyond measure when they are taken and applied to this twentieth century Thomas, this brother of Traherne, this friend who shares himself with us so freely, helping us to discover, even in ourselves,

> that our own life, our part in the universe is infinitely rich, full of inexhaustible interest, opening out into infinite further possibilities for study, contemplation and interest and praise.

This "mind awake in the dark" alerts us ever and again to the presence of God's kingdom with us, amongst us, within us, as his seventeenth century brother says with such emphasis, *"We are in God's kingdom even now."*

Notes and References

1. Thomas Merton, *The Hidden Ground of Love* (ed. Shannon) London, Collins Flame, 1990, p.26

2. Thomas Merton, *Dancing in the Water of Life* —The Journals of Thomas Merton, Vol 5 (ed. Daggy) USA, HarperSanFrancisco, 1997, p.173

3. Ibid.

4. Thomas Merton, *The Other Side of the Mountain* — The Journals of Thomas Merton, Vol 7 (ed. Patrick Hart) USA, HarperSanFrancisco, 1998, p.21

5. Thomas Merton, *The Road to Joy*, (ed. Daggy) NY, Farrar Straus & Giroux 1989, p.62

6. David Ford, *Self and Salvation: Being Transformed.* Cambridge, CUP, 1999, p.276

7. Elizabeth Jennings, *Every Changing Shape*, London, Dent, 1961, pp. 83-4

THOMAS MERTON
a mind awake in the dark

KEYNOTE ADDRESSES

LAWRENCE S. CUNNINGHAM

CHRISTINE M. BOCHEN

DOMINIC WALKER

Thomas Merton
and the Stranger

Lawrence S. Cunningham

> Make the stranger welcome and say something useful.
>
> Evagrius Ponticus, On Asceticism and Stillness

> You are longer strangers and sojourners,
> but you are fellow citizens with the saints
> and members of the household of God.
>
> Ephesians 2:19

HAD THOMAS MERTON LIVED TO EDIT HIS JOURNALS COMPILED DURING his fateful pilgrimage to Asia I am reasonably certain he would not have called the finished product *An Asian Journal*. I say that with some confidence because Merton had a near genius for crafting brilliantly evocative titles for his books. Those titles almost always made a strategic, if sometimes, subtle point. In the case of *The Seven Storey Mountain* it was the strategy of allusion to that most monastic cantica of Dante's *Commedia* with its purgatorial cleansing of the seven deadly sins (or, more properly, the eight *logismoi* described and analyzed by Evagrius of Pontus and John Cassian) accompanied by an increasing shedding of the *pondus* of those sins until one was ready to enter the edenic happiness of the earthly paradise—the symbol of the monastic life as the *paradisus claustralis*. Merton's title, in short, made a dense allusion to Dante's purgatorial journey in particular and, by extension, to Christian ascent literature in general. In *Conjectures of a Guilty Bystander* we catch both the social location of the one who conjectures and the incipient guilt of the one who does the watching from the edges; the bystander is a species of the stranger, a topic this paper will soon make as a specific focus. Perhaps the most brilliant of his titles adorned one of the books with which he found the least satisfaction: *A Vow of Conversation*. In that title is a stunning play of words. Each monk takes a vow of 'conversion of manners' which becomes, in Benedict's curious Latin, *conversatio morum*. Benedict also tells us that the monk needs to cultivate a spirit of silence or, more properly, taciturnity (*taciturnitas*)—an economy of speech. Merton, however, struggled to gain the right to speak and write from the vantage point of the cloister. Hence, his title both alludes to a vow of conversion and a determination to speak—a determination which was the hallmark of his attempt to understand himself as a contemplative from the late 1950s on.

We know from the journals that Merton took care in choosing his titles and, before publication, tinkered with one possibility and another. We know, for instance, that books like *Thoughts in Solitude* and *Seeds of Contemplation* had working titles that were quite different from their final ones. We also know that certain titles, especially of the poetry, are allusive almost to the point of obscurity, as the published research parsing out the significance of *Cables to the Ace* and *The Geography of Lograire* attest. Similarly, we are simply arrested by such eye catching titles as *Raids on the Unspeakable* or *Zen and the Birds of Appetite*. Who can resist the sly title of the 'Cold War Letters' in which, to the insider, the war is not so much between the Soviet Bloc and the West but between Merton and the superior general in Rome.

Which brings me to a consideration of the 1967 essay *Day of a Stranger* published first in the *Hudson Review*—a rather high brow American literary quarterly still alive today. This essay, first written in 1965 when Merton took up residence in his cinder block hermitage, has many characteristics of his writing in the period after the collection *Disputed Questions* (another brilliant title): observations about the world of nature; short imaginary snatches of interior dialogue; brief sketches of the quotidian round of eremitical life; a litany of literary figures; some moments of humor. Juxtapositions of "pious" Trappist tractors growling in the bottoms with the ominous SAC planes flying overhead with their metallic bodies pregnant with bombs.

There is no discernible narrative thread stitching together the essay as a whole. The piece is more like a mosaic, a collection of quick strokes of a sketch, that aims to provide, in the end, a whole. It was the kind of writing Merton had come to love because it provided a formal vehicle for the conveyance of ideas and convictions that increasingly preoccupied him from the late 1950s on.

The very singular style of *Day of a Stranger* comes into sharper relief if one compares it to the account of another day or, more precisely, a single night in the life of the monk: the 'Fire Watch' epilogue to *The Sign of Jonas* written two decades earlier. *Day of a Stranger* is set in the light; the 'Fire Watch' is a meditation on the night. The earlier piece is centered on the monastery and monastic life. Its energy derives from the old mystical *topos* of going down and going up (a leitmotif of the Book of Jonah itself) with its spiritual tone suffused with biblical and liturgical allusions.[1] By contrast, *Day of a Stranger* is horizontal, decentered with respect to the abbey, ironic, hip, and, in places, sly. Its major frame is not the long interval between Compline and Lauds as the community sleeps but between the intervals of arriving and again arriving SAC bombers which never seem to sleep. Its canopy is not the starlit sky embraced from a church tower but the blue sky crosshatched by ominous flying metallic birds.

The monk who wrote 'Fire Watch' was relatively young in the monastic life with the essay being an attempt to recapitulate his monastic life by indirection and reflection. 'Fire Watch' in particular and *The Sign of Jonas* in general is a profoundly and explicitly monastic book. The author of *Day of a Stranger* has had nearly a quarter a century of monastic experience behind him who now had embarked on a new life – or, better: a new stage of life – in the quiet of a hermitage. This mature monk calls himself a "stranger."

My question – and the question to which these reflections address themselves – is this: Who is the Stranger of Merton's title? And further: Stranger to what?

The concept of the stranger is one that carries with it mystery, danger, and possible grace. In an issue of a journal of myth and tradition devoted to the theme of the stranger, the editors noted that one role of the stranger is "to call us to a meeting at the border – the place between ourselves and the 'face of the sky' – where we might discover a kind of knowing that relates not only to place but also to time."[2]

We might then begin to answer the question: "Who is a stranger?"

We might start with the simple observation that in the bible every stranger (*peregrinus*) is an icon of Christ. In the great eschatological sermon in Matthew's Gospel Jesus says "I was a stranger and you welcomed me" (Mt 25:35).[3] More pertinently, for our purposes, we note that the *Rule of Benedict* (Chapter 53) cites that verse from Matthew in its advice on the reception and care of guests who, when they present themselves at the monastery, are to be "welcomed as Christ." The stranger, and hospitality provided to the stranger, is fundamental to monasticism since the stranger is always, in some deep fundamental fashion, the person of Christ. To be hospitable to the stranger is to be hospitable to Christ.

Was it not hospitality, in fact, that the young Thomas Merton experienced when he first approached the monastery to join his life to theirs? The young orphaned wanderer who bounced around France, New York, Bermuda, and England, in fact found his true home when he came to the Gethsemani guest house in December of 1941, as he makes clear in his description of being welcomed into the guest-house when he came to stay.

A curious paradox happens when one joins the monastic community especially if one was first a stranger, rather like the young Tom Merton, looking for a home. Such a stranger receives a welcome as if he were not a stranger but an icon of Christ but then becomes a stranger in a new fashion by the very act of receiving hospitality in the monastery. In that wonderfully titled chapter in the *Rule* named 'Tools for Good Works' Benedict says that the monk, in the very act when he (or she) becomes a monk, makes himself a stranger to the ways of the world, putting Christ before all things.[4] In that brief observation Benedict holds out a vision of the monastic life as a counter-cultural choice in which the monk not only flees the world but also, in that flight, passes judgment on his or her former way of life to embrace a new life—a conversion with its inevitable aversion. There is, in short, a kind of prophetic edge found in the laconic observation in the *Rule*.

Flight from the world (*Fuga mundi*) is a fundamental characteristic of all monasticism. Nonetheless, it is a notion that has a dialectical edge to it. The monk becomes a stranger to the world in a voluntary move and through a style of life but, simultaneously, must learn to love the world with a spirit of compassion and concern. Perhaps the most emblematic example of that dialectic located between flight and concern is the Russian *staretz* who is defined both by his seclusion from the world in a strictly eremitical mode of life in order, in God's good time, to receive the world once again. To use the Russian formulation: the *staretz* "opens his doors" for the world. To put it briefly: monastic flight has, as its counter point, monastic hospitality—the reception of all as if they were Christ coming as stranger.

It may cut close to a banality to observe that the 1950s were a time when Merton tried to sort out and negotiate first for himself, and then with his superiors, how he was to live in flight from the world and yet have compassion for the world. What he most certainly came to see was that a monk could not shape his own culture and his own place in the monastery without regard for the culture in which he lived. If the early monastic tradition had to borrow Donatus on grammar and Cicero on friendship to aid their monastic formation, so the monk of the late modern period could not live a contemplative life wilfully ignorant of either the great masters of suspicions like Freud and Marx (or, at least, the culture they represented) or the valid insights of other contemplative religious traditions. Readers of the journals and books like *The Climate of Monastic Prayer* or the essays in *Contemplation in a World of Action* know all too well how burning this issue was for Merton.

By the late 1950s Merton had come to the firm conclusion that he had a vocation, as a contemplative monk, to speak from that vantage point on the burning issues of the day. The very fact that he had made that decision and began, despite obstacles from both within the Cistercian Order and without, put him in a position not unlike that once described by the theologian Paul Tillich: a person on the margins neither beholden to the traditional role of the monk nor part of the engaged activists who were inspired by the writer whom Merton studied and wrote about with such care: Albert Camus.

We may look back with a certain familiarity at Merton the writer on pacifism, race relations, the struggle for justice in Latin America and the protestor of cold war atomic policies but we do so because of our temptation to put such activists into a single class. However, such reductionism is beside the point. What we must recapture is the strangeness – the singularity – of a contemplative monk so engaged.

One could hardly imagine the kind of writings that Merton did coming from the pen of a Columba Marmion or a Hubert van Zeller or a Eugene Boylan, or even a Raymond Flanagan. Writers in the monastic milieu were expected to write about the life of prayer, not about the critique of social ills. The very topics to which Merton addressed himself shifted him, at least partially, from the central issues of monasticism traditionally understood.

In order for Merton to do the kind of writing that he did, given the seriousness with which he took his commitment to monastic life, he had to find some way to articulate his role as a person on the margins – the person who was a "guilty bystander" or one who launched "raids on the unspeakable" or brought up "disputed questions" – who fully engaged the problems of the world while still affirming himself as one who in the words I quoted earlier from the *Rule of Benedict* took up a life that made him a "stranger to the ways of the world."

One place – among many – where Merton took up that issue of being a stranger to the world explicitly was in his preface to a Japanese translation of *The Seven Storey Mountain*. That introductory statement is justly famous as Merton spoke to an audience that knew little of Christianity in general, and monastic life in particular, about what he meant his life to say. Readers familiar with that classic text in which Merton saw his very life as a statement that both said NO to evil, terror, suppression and persecution while saying YES to all that is good and beautiful will also remember that the monk could only do this were he placed in a certain position *vis à vis* the world. Merton concludes with these words:

> ...for this 'yes' to be an assent of freedom and not of subjection, I must live so that no one of them [i.e. all the men and women of the world] may seem to belong to me, and that I may not belong to any of them. It is because I want to be more to them than a friend that I become, to all of them, a stranger.

Those words deserve some reflection.[5] They could be read as an act of distance by one who lives in the abstract or in a life bereft of human contact but, given the wider reflections that Merton wrote about the role of solitude, monastic withdrawal, locating oneself on the margins for the sake of the contemplative life, it seems more proper to say that the very act of being a monk hermit demands, simultaneously, both distance and intimacy, with the former deriving directly from the life of the monk itself, and the other flowing from that love which comes from embracing the life of contemplation. In other words, his statement is a kind of *apologia* for the monastic life not unlike that made in his exchange of letters with Rosemary Reuther. One should not elide too quickly over the reason for this state of being as an "assent of freedom and not of subjection" since it is that free YES that permits Merton from his solitude to extend love and concern by his writing, his prayer and his solidarity to the world of men and women.

It seems to me that the very compressed remarks Merton makes in that preface was prepared for in his earlier reflections on the meaning of solitude. In an early work like *Thoughts in Solitude* (1956) the emphasis may well be on self possession to avoid the illusions of the world, and the need to listen in silence for the Truth to emerge from nothingness, but the more Merton meditated on solitude the more he saw the solitary as one who lived in solitude in solidarity with all the people of the world. That shift in his thinking is most transparent in an essay which Merton himself thought to be one of his better efforts: 'Philosophy of Solitude.'[6] In that essay Merton consciously links the desire for solitude to the need to escape the illusions of mass society, blinding ideologies, and illusory materialism in order for the solitary to stand, as it were, prophetically against sin in the world in order, as Merton says, to disagree "with those who imagine that the call to diversion [Merton refers to Pascal's *divertissement*] and self-deception is the voice of truth and who can summon the full authority of their prejudices to prove it."

Merton saw the essays in *Disputed Questions* as a new way of writing and a new category of issues to be confronted from the perspective of his evolving understanding of his own monastic vocation. Central to that evolving perspective was plotting out where one stood (metaphorically and existentially) as his exchanges with people as diverse as Joan Baez, the folk singer, and Rosemary Reuther, the theologian, make clear: he did not, and could not, forsake his vocation for the role of the activist. He continued to examine the role of the person on the margin, the outsider, the stranger, and the solitary in relation to the great social issues of the day.

That ongoing evolution is patent when one considers the informal address[7] that Merton gave in Calcutta a month before his death.

Speaking to a decidedly interreligious group connected to the Temple of Understanding, Merton focused on his understanding of the role of the monk in the contemporary world. In those remarks he describes the monk as a "marginal person," a "status-less person," a "strange" person, who is as "irrelevant" as the poet or the hippie or the prisoner. This marginal person goes through the "Great Doubt" precisely because the monk is a person of faith who must face the other side of faith, which is doubt. He sums up such a way of being as characteristic of those "people who dare to seek on the margin of society, who are not dependent on social acceptance, not dependent on social routine, and prefer a kind of free-floating existence under a state of risk."

Now comes a bit of a paradox and it is this: if such people are faithful to their calling they discover at the deepest level possible not only communication but communion which is, in Merton's phrasing of it, "beyond words" and "beyond speech" and finally "beyond concepts." The paradox, of course, is that the very situation of marginality and strangeness brings at a deep level not alienation but communion. Although the language and the conceptual framework is quite different, the dynamic is not all that different from what entrance into the monastic way brings: one embraces monastic hospitality, which makes one alien to the world only to bring one to a sense of compassion for the world, just as marginality and lack of status brings a deep unity and not mere communication but communion.

One could not reflect on the stranger in Merton's thinking without making reference to his intense study of Albert Camus whom he refers to in passing in *A Day of a Stranger* as an "Algerian cenobite". Merton's study of Camus, a study which occupied a fair amount of his energies from the fall of 1966 through the following year, resulted in a monograph length series of essays.[8] There are two reasons why Merton would have been attracted to Camus. First, Camus was an "outsider" in many ways: an Algerian by birth; a dissident as far as the orthodox existentialists (if that is the word) represented by Jean-Paul Sartre and the circle of *Les Temps Modernes* were concerned; a critic of Marxist orthodoxy while remaining a man of the Left.

Second, Merton had a profound respect for Francophone intellectual culture in general, and in particular he loved the emphasis that Camus put on integrity, honesty, and on the demand for lucidity in the face of exigent realities in the world and in culture. Merton appreciated that Camus, unlike Sartre, was not one who set his face in stone against the claims of religious faith. Camus examined them, and not unlike Merton although from a vastly different perspective, demanded that believers not comfort themselves with illusions in the name of orthodoxy. Most of all, Camus demanded that people face up to the evil of the world and fight against it even though in their lucidity they knew that evil in this life would always be part of the fabric of existence.

What Thomas Merton learned from his study of Camus was that the person of authentic lucidity (how Merton loved that quintessentially existentialist word "lucidity"!) was one who went beyond the illusions of ideology and self-regard in order to live a life of authenticity. To do that, as Camus argued in works like *The Rebel* and *The Plague*, one had to stand apart from the temptations of the crowd and, more tellingly, from those who wished to direct the energies of the crowd. As Merton wrote (discussing *The Plague*): an ethic of such comprehension

> is almost a monastic ascesis; it demands constant attention (compare the old monastic 'vigilance' and 'custody of the heart'). It is a monastic spirituality of exile because he who refuses to co-operate with the 'pestilence' which is part and parcel of every social establishment cannot be really accepted by that establishment.[9]

Such a life always put one in a state of tension with the majority. The tension involves being concerned with, but always somewhat apart from, the social majority. This was a theme that Merton also articulated in his essay 'Rain and the Rhinoceros' even though in that study it was the Romanian playwright Eugene Ionesco whose play *The Rhinoceros* became the the subject of his meditation. Merton, recalling the insights of the sixth century hermit Philoxenos (who saw the Christ of the desert taking on the loneliness and destitution of every person) remarked that today when regarding the loneliness and human alienation the "insights of a Philoxenos are to be sought less in the tracts of theologians than in the meditations of the existentialists and in the theatre of the absurd."[10]

To trace the image of the Stranger we have followed a broad arc that moves from the *Rule of Benedict* through the experience(s) of Merton's own development as a monk to his life in the hermitage and his quiet meetings with the mind of people like Albert Camus and Eugene Ionesco. The one constant in this trajectory is a certain tension or distance between the person who is the stranger and the world from which he or she is estranged. We have tried to parse out that distance in these pages.

What is left to do is to take one last look at the stranger as the one who comes and whom we meet in such a way that they are not only strangers but welcome guests. This is a very ancient theme in the sacred scriptures. It is the theme behind Abraham's hospitality at the oaks of Mambre (Gen 18) and it is crystalized in the haunting affirmation of the high Egyptian official who greets the famine driven Jews with the poignantly loving confession "I am Joseph your brother..." (Gen 45: 4). It is that same recognition and erasure of distance which reveals the stranger on the road to Emmaus to be the Risen One who is recognized in that act of hospitality which is the breaking of the bread (Lk 24: 31).

The erasure of distance between host and stranger is, of course, what monastic hospitality is all about—the welcoming of the stranger by the monastic strangers in the name of Christ. The *Sayings of the Desert Fathers* recount many instances of the stranger becoming an honored guest. When people came to seek the hospitality of the desert dwellers they most commonly came with a request ("Abba, give me a good word") or a question ("Abba, What must I do?"). It is not a rhetorical flourish on my part to stipulate that more than thirty years after his death we query that stranger in the cinder block hermitage on the hill with very similar words: "Father Louis, give me a good word." And, he always does.

Notes and References

1. I have parsed many of these allusions in 'Thomas Merton: Firewatcher,' *The Merton Seasonal* xv (Spring, 1990) 6-11.
2. Ellen Dooling Harper and Virginia Baron. 'Focus' in *Parabola* XX/2 (1995) - an introduction to a special issue devoted to 'The Stranger.'
3. The concept of "stranger" has a complex history in the bible. The stranger can mean one who is not a member of a social group (in that sense it was applied to Abraham, Moses, and the Israelites in Egypt) or, after the settlement, it meant resident aliens in the promised land to whom social obligations were due; see: Ex 22:21; Deut 10:19.

4. *Saeculi actibus se facere alienum* is translated in the Timothy Fry edition (Liturgical Press, 1981) as "your way of acting should be different from the world's way" which strikes me as flaccid.

5. The entire preface is reproduced in *Honorable Reader: Reflections on My Work*, ed. Robert E. Daggy (New York: Crossroad, 1989) 64-67; see especially 65-66.

6. In *Disputed Questions* (New York: Farrar, Straus & Cudahy, 1960) 177-207. I consider that essay in detail in Lawrence S. Cunningham *Thomas Merton and the Monastic Vision* (Grand Rapids,MI: Eerdmans, 1999) 77-79.

7. Reproduced in the first appendix of *Asian Journal* (New York: New Directions, 1973)

8. Those essays (seven in all) are available in *The Literary Essays of Thomas Merton*, edited by Patrick Hart (New York: New Directions, 1981) 181-304.

9. *Literary Essays* 206.

10. 'Rain and the Rhinoceros' was first published in *Holiday* magazine (1965) and then reprinted in *Raids on the Unspeakable* (1996); I quote from the anthology *Thomas Merton: Spiritual Master*, ed. Lawrence S. Cunningham (New York: Paulist, 1992) 395. The very name "Philoxenos", of course, means "love of the stranger."

Radiant Darkness:
The Dawning into Reality

CHRISTINE M. BOCHEN

THE TITLE FOR MY TALK, "'Radiant Darkness': Dawning into Reality," is inspired, as is the theme of this meeting, by Thomas Merton's *Day of a Stranger*. *Day of a Stranger* offers readers insight into Thomas Merton— as a contemplative, social critic, and poet who, in the radiant darkness of contemplation, awakens to the light of Reality. Merton wrote *Day of a Stranger* in response to an invitation from Ludovico Silva, a South American editor who was thinking of doing a book on a day in the life of poets. As was often the case with Merton's articles and essays, *Day of a Stranger* underwent several revisions and expansions. On the cover page of the third draft, Merton hand wrote the note:

> These pages were written in answer to a request from a South American editor to describe a 'typical day' in my life. The day was sometime in May 1965. Since then this has been rewritten & slightly amplified.

Before discussing the final version, published in the United States, I want to set the "typical day" which Merton describes in *Day of a Stranger* in the context of Merton's days in May, 1965.

May 1965: A View from Merton's Journal

For years Merton had longed for the solitude of the hermitage, glorying in those all-too-brief interludes when he was able to retreat to the woodshed, which he affectionately named St. Anne's, or disappear, for a few hours, into the nearby woods. In August 1965, Merton would begin living full time in the hermitage. But this was May, and he was moving back and forth between the hermitage and the monastery, spending as much time as he was able in the hermitage. He was still expected to be present at the monastery for liturgy, for conferences he was giving to the novices, and for a meal with the community. Nevertheless, Merton was relishing his newly found freedom. Life in the hermitage was full of joy for him, but he soon learned that living alone was not free of demands. Merton found that the tasks of housekeeping and food preparation could be burdensome on occasion and he even complained about the effort that living alone required. For example, in January 1965, on the vigil of his fiftieth birthday, he interrupted more serious reflections with the observation that "work takes up so much time and there can be so much. Just keeping the place clean is already a big task. Then there is the wood to be chopped." I must admit that there is a part of me that took great delight in Merton's observations on the joys of house-keeping! In the years to come, he would discover that living in solitude could entail more serious hardships and challenges. But, in May 1965, we find Merton celebrating the blessings afforded by his solitary life and deeply grateful that he was able to spend much of his day in the hermitage.

Merton's journal entries for May – there are ten in all – allow us to glimpse what his life was like and, as might be expected, to preview themes that surface in *Day of a Stranger*.[1] In the first entry, we note Merton's close attention to his natural environment. On May 1, 1965, Merton writes:

> Perfectly beautiful spring weather – sky utterly cloudless all day – birds singing all around the hermitage—deep green grass. When I am here, all the time towhees and tanagers are at peace, not worried, and with their constant singing I always know where they are. It is a wonderful companionship to have them constantly within the very small circle of woods which is their area and mine—where they have their nests and I have mine. Sometimes the woodthrush comes, but only on special occasions like the evening of St Robert's day. Last evening I interrupted my meditation to watch a half a dozen savannah sparrows outside my bedroom.[2]

This journal entry, like countless others, invites us into Merton's world as he evokes a sense of the place in which he lives. But his journal entries also record what he is writing, reading and doing.

Early in May 1965, Merton finishes the first draft of an essay called 'Contemplation and Ecumenism.' He reports that he is working on Chuang Tzu, and by month's end, he has finished his renderings of Chuang Tzu and is "exhilarated by the effect of all of them."[3] He is pleased to receive a Catalan translation of *Black Revolution*—which has already appeared in French, English and German.[4]

Laid low by a "bug," Merton spends a couple days in the infirmary reading Martin Ling's *Ancient Beliefs and Modern Superstitions,* "a good chunk" of Volume I of De Lubac's *Exégèse médiévale,* and Herbert Read's *Green Child.* Of these, he notes that De Lubac was "the most exciting."[5] Later in the month, he notes that he has finished De Lubac's book and has "a good little book on Camus." When he recovers from the "bug," he has visitors, including Jay Laughlin with whom he goes to see Victor Hammer; a priest and an architect working on the design of a new Poor Clare Monastery in Chicago who came to Gethsemani seeking Merton's advice; Sister Mary Luke Tobin, a Loretto sister and one of two women observers appointed to the Second Vatican Council, with whom he discusses the revised Schema of Religious; Dom Philip, a Benedictine Prior from California, from whom Merton hears about monasticism in·Africa. Merton is anticipating visits from Zalman Schachter, Dan Berrigan and Jim Douglass. During the month he also wrote twenty-one letters to correspondents—among them D.T. Suzuki, Etta Gullick, Ernesto Cardenal, Jim Forest, Pope Paul VI, Daniel Berrigan, James Douglas, A. M. Allchin, and Clayton Eshleman.

But Merton's hours were not all filled with activity. As was his practice, he spent many hours in silence and prayer. Words of scripture – he was reading Ecclesiasticus in the Latin Septuagint – speak to his heart. Reading "The Lord has plucked up proud men by their roots, and planted the lowly in their place," (Ecc. 10:18 [15]), Merton thinks

> If I were more fully attentive to the word of God I would be much less troubled and disturbed by the events of our time: not that I would be indifferent or passive, but I could gain the strength of union with the deepest currents in history, the sacred currents which run opposite to those on the surface a great deal of the time![6]

He feels the need for "'attention' and 'listening,' for I have come to the most serious moments of my life."[7] And he experiences moments of deep peace:

> one lovely dawn after another. Such peace! Meditation with fireflies, mist in the valley, last quarter of the moon, distant owls—gradual inner awakening and centering in peace and harmony of love and gratitude.[8]

But there is no peace in the world. Merton hears rumors that President Johnson is claiming to have discovered Communist missile bases in Santo Domingo and is sending in the Marines. He is disturbed by an article on 'Escalation' by Herbert Kahn, which Merton thinks is full of "technological doubletalk" that ignores the fact that people, millions of people, could die in a nuclear event. Kahn "explicitly treats various 'reasonable' ways in which all kinds of 'conventional' acts of war and harassment, and also nuclear weapons, can and may be used 'for bargaining'" and speaks of "'slow motion counter property war,' 'constrained force reduction salvo,' 'constrained disarming attack,' then of course 'slow motion countercity war' in which the game becomes 'city trading' – a nice 'test of nerves'" – all "'practicable'" as long as it is "'controlled.'"[9] And Merton remarks

> the word control will be enough to convince a number of Catholic theologians and bishops that this is a perfectly legitimate application of double effect. The moral theology of hell!! What bastards![10]

On May 22, 1965, he writes,

> Grey dawn. A blood red sun, furious among the pines (it will soon be hidden in clouds). That darn black hound is baying in the hollow after some rabbit he will never catch. Deep grass in the field, dark green English woods (for we have had good rains). The bombing goes on in Viet Nam. The whole thinking of this country is awry on war: basic conviction that force is the only thing that is effective.[11]

The natural landscape with its greyness, blood red sun, and baying hound mirrors a disturbed national psyche. Still his solitude is full of promise:

> Whole day at the hermitage. I have come to see that only these days in solitude are really full and 'whole' for me. The others are partly wasted.

All of this tells us something about what Merton's life was like in May 1965—not simply by reporting what he was doing and thinking but by drawing attention to the mix of silence and activity which reveals both Merton's desire for solitude and his engagement in the world. This was the context in which Merton wrote the first two versions of Day of a Stranger. Later when he was living full time in the hermitage, Merton revised and expanded what he had written in May 1965.

Day of a Stranger

Three versions of Day of a Stranger have been published. The first version, Merton's original draft, was only four pages long. It has been published in *Dancing in the Water of Life*, Volume 5 of Thomas Merton's journals.[12] Merton sent the second version, revised and expanded to eight and one-half pages, to Ludovico Silva. Merton had written and rewritten the piece quickly: Silva enthusiastically acknowledged receipt of 'Day of a Stranger' in a letter dated June 2, 1965. Silva's wife, Rosita, translated the piece into Spanish. Although the book on days in the lives of poets which Silva had planned never came to be – Merton was the only poet who responded – 'Dia de un Extraño' was published in Caracas, in the first issue (July-August-September 1966) of a literary magazine entitled *Papeles*.[13] Merton reworked the text of 'Day of a Stranger,' which he had sent to Latin America, to produce a revised and expanded third version of 'Day of a Stranger.'[14] The final eleven-page typescript of 'Day of a Stranger,' as it was published in the USA differs only slightly from the third version.[15] 'Day of a Stranger' was accepted for publication in the *Hudson Review* on December 14, 1966 and appeared in the Summer 1967 issue of the magazine. In 1981, Robert E. Daggy published *Day of a Stranger* as a handsome, small book with a selection of Merton's photographs and a fine introduction.[16]

Speaking to a Latin American Audience

Merton opens the first draft with lines which he retains through all the revisions: "The hills are blue and hot. There is a brown, dusty field in the bottom of the valley. I hear a machine, a bird, a clock. The clouds are high and enormous."[17] Looking up he sees a jet probably on its way from Chicago to Miami and recalls that he has also seen "the plane with the bomb in it" flying over him.[18] "Like everyone else I live under the bomb. But unlike most people I live in the woods."[19] Merton goes on to describe the mental ecology – "a mental balance of spirits" – in his corner of the woods, contrasting it with the non-ecology or unbalance of the world around him. This is a passage Robert E. Daggy had in mind when he characterized Merton's first draft as "short, terse, angry."[20] The passage, which Merton deleted when he revised the piece, reveals Merton's intense frustration with American society as well as his strong identification with Latin America. Merton writes:

there is the non-ecology, the destructive unbalance of nature, poisoned and unsettled by bombs, by fallout, by exploitation: the land ruined, the waters contaminated, the soil charged with chemicals, ravaged with machinery, the houses of farmers falling apart because everybody goes to the city and stays there... There is no poverty so great as that of the prosperous, no wretchedness so dismal as affluence. Wealth is poison. There is no misery to compare with that which exists where technology has been a total success. I know that these are hard sayings, and that they are unbearable when they are said in other countries where so many lack everything. But do you imagine that if you become prosperous as the United States you will no longer have needs? Here the needs are even greater. Full bellies have not brought peace and satisfaction but dementia, and in any case not all bellies are full either. But the dementia is the same for all.[21]

In another passage, Merton reports that as he goes down into the valley and sees the field where the monks are planting corn, he is deeply moved:

After dawn I go down into the valley, first under the pines, then under tall oaks, then down a sharp incline, past an old barn, out into the field where they are now planting corn. Later in the summer the corn will be tall and sacred and the wind will whisper through the thousands of leaves and stalks as if all the spirits of the Maya were there. I weep in the corn for what was done in past ages, in the carnage that brought America the dignity of having a 'history.' I live alone with blood of the Indians on my head.[22]

Looking back into the past and aware of the present, Merton sees a nation intent upon ruin and destruction; blind to reality; powerful and immoral—a nation in which he is a stranger.

Soon I will cut bread, eat supper, say psalms, sit in the back room as the sun sets, as the birds sing outside the window, as silence descends on the valley, as night descends. As night descends on a nation intent upon ruin, upon destruction, blind, deaf to protest, crafty, powerful, unintelligent. It is necessary to be alone, to be not part of this, to be in the exile of silence, to be in a manner of speaking a political prisoner. No matter where in the world he may be, no matter what may be his power of protest, or his means of expression, the poet finds himself ultimately where I am. Alone, silent, with the obligation of being very careful not to say what he does not mean, not to let himself be persuaded to say merely what another wants him to say, not to say, what his own past work has led others to expect him to say. The poet has to be free from everyone else, and first of all from himself, because it is through this "self" that he is captured by others.

> Freedom is found under the dark tree that springs up in the center of night and of silence, the paradise tree, the axis mundi, which is also the Cross.[23]

As monk and poet, he is a stranger.

'Day of a Stranger' is not the first piece Merton wrote for a Latin American audience. In 1961, he wrote 'A Letter to Pablo Antonio Cuadra concerning Giants' in which he decried the abominable behavior of the superpowers – the United States and the Soviet Union – who flagrantly abuse their power—economic in the case of the USA, and political in the case of the USSR. In letters to his numerous Latin American correspondents, Merton spoke often and eloquently of his sense of kinship with Latin American writers and his strong sense of identification with Latin American people. He was hopeful that writers and poets – who speak the truth – would be a force for life in Latin America and that Latin America will be the hope of the world.[24] Merton's preface to the Spanish translation of *The Complete Works of Thomas Merton*, written in 1958 and published in *Honorable Reader*, echoes these sentiments.[25]

As he revised the first draft, Merton tempered his anger and softened his tone. Robert E. Daggy observed that Merton "became less concerned with conveying his message of danger and destruction and more concerned with relating the messages he received during the day—much the same message, of course, but the mood shifts."[26] One passage, which Merton deleted from the version of 'Day of a Stranger' published in Latin America as he expanded the piece for publication in America, elaborates on his identity as a stranger. Following the statement – "I live in the woods as a reminder that I am free not to be a number. There is, in fact, a choice." – Merton had written:

> I do not intend to belong to the world of squares that is constituted by the abdication of choice; or be the fraudulent choice (the mass-roar in the public square or the assent to the televised grimace).

> I do not intend to be citizen number 152037. I do not consent to be poet number 2291. I do not recognize myself as the classified anti-social and subversive element that I probably am in the file of a department in a department. Perhaps I have been ingested by an IBM machine in Washington, but they cannot digest me. I am indigestible: a priest who cannot be swallowed, a monk notoriously discussed as one of the problems of the contemporary Church by earnest seminarists, wearing bright spectacles in Rome.

I have not chosen to be acceptable. I have not chosen to be inacceptable. I have nothing personal to do with the present indigestion of officials, of critics, of clerics, of housewives, of amateur sociologists. It is their indigestion. I offer them no advice.[27]

Citizen, poet, monk, priest—Merton is the alien, the stranger, the marginal person.

'Day of a Stranger,' revised and expanded for publication in Latin America and once again for publication in the United States, becomes subtler and more effective as Merton's spiritual vision informs the text in a more explicit way.

Day of a Stranger: Merton's Spiritual Vision

Merton had been invited to write about a day in the life of a poet. He did that and more as he revealed himself as poet and monk – and a special kind of monk at that – a hermit, living alone in the woods. *Day of a Stranger* not only succeeds in portraying "a day" in Merton's life but also in drawing a richly nuanced portrait of Merton in his simplicity *and* complexity. *Day of a Stranger* allows us to glimpse something of the many facets of Merton's life and of his many interests. All the themes that define Merton's life and writing in the mid- and late sixties are evident in *Day of a Stranger*, where we encounter the contemplative, the social critic, and the poet. Merton's incisive critique of contemporary culture, his passion for peace, his sense of rootedness in the world of nature, his company of intellectual and spiritual soul mates – all are in evidence in *Day of a Stranger* – all rooted in his contemplative spirituality. Merton's contemplative vision frames and grounds *Day of a Stranger* just as his contemplative spirituality framed and grounded his life.

At the center of *Day of a Stranger* is a passage that expresses Merton's contemplative practice and provides a glimpse of the vision that flows from contemplation. In this passage, Merton describes how he rises in the darkness of night to pray the psalms of the Liturgy of the Hours and rest in the silence of night. Light breaks in: first, the candlelight; then, the light of truth spoken in psalms; finally, in silence, God's word of mercy – great mercy – a word which cleanses Merton, purifies him, and makes him whole. The silence of the night is broken by words of prayer and the words heard in prayer draw him into a deeper silence. So it is that the darkness of night becomes radiant with light. Once more Reality dawns and, in its radiant light, Merton sees through illusion.

> I am out of bed at two-fifteen in the morning when the night is darkest and most silent...I find myself in the primordial lostness of night, solitude, forest, peace, a mind awake in the dark, looking for a light, not totally reconciled to being out of bed. A light appears, and in the light an icon. There is now in the large darkness a small room of radiance with psalms in it. The psalms grow up silently by themselves without effort like plants in this light which is favorable to them. The plants hold themselves up on stems which have a single consistency, that of mercy, or rather great mercy. *Magna misericordia.* In the formlessness of night and silence a word then pronounces itself: Mercy. It is surrounded by other words of lesser consequence: "destroy iniquity" "wash me" "purify" "I know my iniquity." *Peccavi.* Concepts without interest in the world of business, war, politics, culture, etc. Concepts also often without interest to ecclesiastics.
>
> Other words: Blood. Guile. Anger. The way that is not good. The way of blood, guile, anger, war.
>
> Out there the hills in the dark lie southward. The way over the hills is blood, guile, dark, anger, death, Selma, Birmingham, Mississippi. Nearer than these, the atomic city, from which each day a freight car of fissionable material is brought to be laid carefully beside the gold in the underground vault which is at the heart of this nation.
>
> "Their mouth is the opening of the grave; their tongues are set in motion by lies; their heart is void."
>
> Blood, lies, fire, hate, the opening of the grave, void. Mercy, great mercy.[28]

And then Merton adds.

> The birds begin to wake. It will soon be dawn. In an hour or two the towns will wake, and men will enjoy everywhere the great luminous smiles of production and business.[29]

In this passage, Merton describes how he prays in the middle of the night—with words and without them. In darkness radiant with light, he sees, with striking clarity, the Reality within and, in the light of the interior vision, he recognizes what others cannot. Observing what is happening in Selma and Birmingham, in Mississippi and in Vietnam, Merton speaks a prophetic word— naming the way of death for what it is and contrasting it with the way of mercy. "Blood, lies, fire, hate, the opening of the grave, void.

Mercy, great mercy."[30] "Mercy, great mercy" is at once a prayer in the face of darkness and a promise of forgiveness and life.

Day of a Stranger is full of contrasts: darkness and light, light breaking into the darkness. Day of a Stranger portrays contrasting worlds: Merton's world, with its ecology, interdependence, balance, harmony, is contrasted with the world beyond the hermitage—a world that intrudes with its sounds of jets and the Strategic Air Command plane with the bomb in it. While Merton knows the precise pairs of birds with whom he shares the woods, the metal bird with a scientific egg in its breast, threatening death, flies overhead. Balance and unbalance!

Mindful of the critters with whom he shares the woods, Merton recognizes the natural ecology in which he has a place. But Merton is also aware of the people who are present with him in his solitude constituting "a mental ecology...a living balance of spirits in this corner of the woods" where there is room "for many other songs besides those of the birds." Mindful of their presence Merton invokes their names—as in a litany of praise gathering in the writers who are so much a part of his own spirit and who are for him a life-giving community.

> Of Vallejo, for instance. Or Rilke, or René Char, Montale and Zukofsky, Ungaretti, Edwin Muir and Quasimondo or some Greeks. Or the dry, disconcerting voice of Nicanor Parra, the poet of the sneeze. Here also is Chuang Tzu whose climate is perhaps most the climate of this silent corner of the woods. A climate in which there is not need for explanation. Here is the reassuring companionship of many silent Tzu's and Fu's; Kung Tzu, Lao Tzu, Meng Tzu, Tu Fu. And Hui Neng. And Chao-Chu. And the drawings of Sengai. And a big graceful scroll from Suzuki. Here also is a Syrian hermit called Philoxenus. An Algerian cenobite called Camus. Here is the challenging prose of Tertullian, with the dry catarrh of Sartre. Here the voluble dissonances of Auden, with the golden sounds of John of Salisbury. Here is the deep vegetation of that more ancient forest in which the angry birds, Isaias and Jeremias, sing. Here should be, and are, feminine voices from Angela of Foligno to Flannery O'Connor, Theresa of Avila, Juliana of Norwich, and, more personally and warmly still, Raïssa Maritain. It is good to choose the voices that will be heard in these woods, but they also choose themselves, and send themselves to be present in this silence. In any case, there is no lack of voices.[31]

The voices of men and women that fill his space are real for Merton. He hears them as voices present in the silence. Together, they form a community that Merton experiences in solitude.

Merton's solitude is radical. He is committed to a celibate life. With wry humor, Merton observes that

> All monks, as is well known, are unmarried and hermits more unmarried than the rest of them. Not that I have anything against women...One might say I had decided to marry the silence of the forest. The sweet dark warmth of the whole world will have to be my wife. Out of the heart of that dark warmth comes the secret that is only heard in silence, but it is the root of all the secrets that are whispered by all the lovers in their beds all over the world. So perhaps I have an obligation to preserve the stillness, the silence, the poverty, the virginal point of pure nothingness which is at the center of all other loves. I attempt to cultivate this plant without comment in the middle of the night and water it with psalms and prophecies in silence.[32]

In stillness, silence and solitude, he encounters the Reality which is at the Center. Although this encounter with the divine Reality in darkness is at the center of his apophatic spirituality, it important to note that Merton awakens to the sacred in the midst of the ordinary. The ordinary things of this world have a place in Merton's spirituality.

> It is necessary for me to see the first point of light which begins to be dawn. It is necessary to be present alone at the resurrection of Day, in the blank silence when the sun appears. In this completely neutral instant I receive from the Eastern woods, the tall oaks, the one word "day," which is never the same. It is never spoken in any known language.[33]

It is necessary to have a sense of place and a sense of time. It is necessary to be present to the day and attentive to the day's simple rituals—rituals that range from washing the coffeepot to addressing the king snake that has taken up residence in the outhouse. "Are you there, you bastard?" Merton asks. He sprays the bedroom. He closes all the windows on the south side, remembering to open those on the north side. He gets the water bottle, the rosary, and the watch. And when it is "time to visit the human race"[34] he walks to the monastery, noticing what he sees along the way and realizing that he has duties and obligations to perform there. Then, during the chanting of the Divine Office, as the monks chant the alleluia, he suddenly hears "only the one note. *Consonantia*: all notes, in their perfect distinctness, are yet blended into one."[35]

Later, in the afternoon, he returns to that one note:

> I sit in the cool back room, where words cease to resound, where all meanings are absorbed in the *consonantia* of heat, fragrant pine, quiet

wind, bird song and one central tonic note that is unheard and unuttered. This is no longer a time of obligations. In the silence of the afternoon all is present and all is inscrutable in one central tonic note to which every other sound ascends or descends, to which every other meaning aspires, in order to find it true fulfillment. To ask when the note will sound is to lose the afternoon: it has already sounded, and all things now hum with the resonance of its sounding.[36]

Hearing the one note—which is unheard and unuttered, Merton is aware, present and awake. The "one note" that sounds in *consonantia* is an encounter with Reality. On May 23, 1965, Merton noted in his journal that he had responded to a letter from a man at Magill University "who thought all contemplation was a manifestation of narcissistic regression!" But Merton wrote, "That is just what it is not." Rather, contemplation is

A complete awakening of identity and of rapport! It implies an awareness, an acceptance of one's place in the whole. First the whole of creation, then the whole plan of Redemption—to find oneself in the great mystery of fulfillment which is the Mystery of Christ. *Consonantia* [harmony] and not *confusio* [confusion].[37]

In the solitude of the hermitage, Merton glimpses that wholeness and harmony that informs all reality. Then he returns to his daily tasks—sweeping, cutting grass, writing, making the bed, and eating supper. Once again he prays the psalms. As night descends,

I become surrounded once again by all the silent Tzu's and Fu's (men without office and without obligation). The birds draw closer to their nests. I sit on the cool straw mat on the floor, considering the bed in which I will presently sleep alone under the ikon of the Nativity.

Meanwhile, the metal cherub of apocalypse passes over me in the clouds, treasuring its egg and its message.[38]

So ends the *Day of a Stranger*.

Dawning into Reality

In *Day of a Stranger*, Merton draws us into his world and, in so doing, he teaches us how to live in our world. He calls us to enter into the radiant darkness and to let Reality dawn within us and within our world. He invites us to recognize the stranger beside us and the stranger within us. He calls us to awaken with him, to become minds "awake in the dark" through prayer and contemplation and solitude and silence.

He invites us to see things for what they are, to use language honestly honoring true meaning, to resist social manipulation, to live in harmony with nature and work to restore the ecological balance. He calls us to nurture a sense of place, a sense of time, a sense of connection, a sense of the present, a sense of mercy, a sense of hidden wholeness and harmony. He calls us to embrace reality. To do so, we must shed illusions about the world and, most of all, about ourselves, as Merton did. In the radiant darkness, he came to see himself as he was. In 1963, he wrote these words of comfort to his dying friend Jacques Maritain:

> Dear Jacques, you are going on your journey to God. And perhaps I am too, though I suppose my eagerness to go is pretty wishful thinking for there is yet work to be done in my own life. There are great illusions to be gotten rid of and there is a false self that has to be taken off if it can be done. There is still much to change before I will really be living in the truth and in nothingness and in humility without any self-concern.[39]

Less than two years later, on the vigil of his fiftieth birthday Merton wrote again about his need to be free:

> What I find most in my whole life is *illusion*. Wanting to be something of which I had formed a concept. I hope I will get free of that now, because that is going to be the struggle. And yet I have to be something that I ought to be—I have to meet a certain demand for order and inner light and tranquility.[40]

Yes, there were illusions in Merton's life as there are in ours. But there was a fundamental truth to his life because he knew the Truth. He came to know Truth as he awakened to radiant darkness and in that darkness to Reality.

Notes and References

1. Merton wrote in his journal on May 1, 10, 11, 15, 20, 22, 23, 25, 28, and 30. See *Dancing in the Water of Life*, ed. by Robert E. Daggy (San Francisco: HarperSanFrancisco, 1997),
2. *Dancing in the Water of Life*, 245.
3. *Dancing in the Water of Life*, 252. Merton's Chuang Tzu poems were published as *The Way of Chuang Tzu* (New York: New Directions, 1965).
4. Several of Merton's essays were published in May 1965 including "Rain and the Rhinoceros."
5. *Dancing in the Water of Life*, 246.
6. *Dancing in the Water of Life*, 248.

7. Dancing in the Water of Life, 248.
8. Dancing in the Water of Life, 250.
9. Dancing in the Water of Life. 245.
10. Dancing in the Water of Life, 245-246.
11. Dancing in the Water of Life, 249.
12. Dancing in the Water of Life, 239-242.
13. "Dia de un Extraño," Papeles 1 (July-August-September 1966), 41-45. Unpublished letters from Ludovico Silva to Thomas Merton, dated May 26, 1966 and June 2, 1966 establish the circumstances of publication. Merton's letters to Silva appear in The Courage for Truth, ed. by Christine M. Bochen (New York: Farrar, Straus & Giroux, 1993), 223-232. I am grateful to Ginny Bear for her translation of the Silva letters.
14. This third version with Merton's handwritten and typed corrections and insertions is housed in the Thomas Merton Center, Bellarmine University, Louisville, Kentucky.
15. Several paragraphs, which Merton retained from version two and several lines he added to version three, were deleted from this final version. This typescript is also housed at the Thomas Merton Center, Bellarmine University, Louisville, Kentucky.
16. Day of a Stranger (Salt Lake City: Gibbs M. Smith/A Peregrine Book, 1981), 63 pages. "Day of A Stranger," the third and final version, has been reprinted in Thomas Merton Spiritual Master, ed. Lawrence Cunningham (New York: Paulist, 1992).
17. First draft of "Day of a Stranger," Dancing in the Water of Life, 239.
18. First draft of "Day of a Stranger," Dancing in the Water of Life, 239.
19. First draft of "Day of a Stranger," Dancing in the Water of Life, 239.
20. Robert E. Daggy, Introduction to Day of a Stranger, 17.
21. First draft of "Day of a Stranger," Dancing in the Water of Life, 240.
22. First draft of "Day of a Stranger," Dancing in the Water of Life, 241.
23. Second draft of "Day of a Stranger." Typescript in the Thomas Merton Center, Bellarmine University. Cited by Robert E. Daggy in Introduction to Day of a Stranger, 18-19.
24. For Merton's letters to Ernesto Cardenal and a host of other Latin American writers and poets, see The Courage for Truth.
25. Thomas Merton, "Preface to the Argentine Edition of The Complete Works of Thomas Merton," "Honorable Reader": Reflections on My Work, ed. Robert E. Daggy (New York: Crossroad, 1989), 35-44.
26. Day of a Stranger, 19.
27. Second draft of "Day of a Stranger." Typescript in the Thomas Merton Center, Bellarmine University. Cited by Robert E. Daggy in Introduction to Day of a Stranger, 20.
28. Day of a Stranger, 43-45.
29. Day of a Stranger, 45.
30. Day of a Stranger, 45.
31. Day of a Stranger, 35-37.
32. Day of a Stranger, 49. Merton speaks of this "virginal point of pure nothingness as "le point vierge." For example, see Thomas Merton, Conjectures of a Guilty Bystander (New York: Doubleday, 1966), 158.
33. Day of a Stranger, 51.

34. *Day of a Stranger*, 53.
35. *Day of a Stranger*, 59.
36. *Day of a Stranger*, 61,
37. *Dancing in the Water of Life*, 250.
38. *Day of a Stranger*, 63.
39. *The Courage for Truth*, 39.
40. *Dancing in the Water of Life*, 198.

Sharing Our Faith Journey:
For Merton there is no Stranger

Dominic Walker ogs

Introduction

THOMAS MERTON WAS RECENTLY DESCRIBED AS 'arguably the most significant writer of the western Christian tradition in the second half of the 20th century'; and for spiritual writings to become real for us we need to know something about the personal spiritual journey of the writer. Indeed, spiritual writings receive their authority and credibility when linked with a personal testimony. I want to suggest that the reason for Thomas Merton's popularity is that his own personal spiritual life and struggle passed through various stages of development which reflect in some degree the various stages within our own spiritual lives. In other words, we can all relate to Merton because he recorded his own spiritual journey in great detail and with such honesty and integrity that we feel that we have been there – or we are at that stage – or if we are not, that we can see, if somewhat dimly, and maybe even resistantly, the likely way ahead.

In exploring the various stages of faith development in Merton's life, I want to draw on some of the insights of the psychology of religion and in particular the writings of James Fowler, who himself drew on some of the insights of Piaget, Erikson and Kohlberg's account of moral development. Whilst critical questions can be raised about the methodology, interpretation and subjectivity of these psychologists and educationalists, if there are indeed discernible stages in faith development, then this may help us to understand Merton and ourselves and also have a bearing on spiritual direction.

James Fowler and Faith Development

James Fowler was a professor of theology and human development who interviewed 359 people ranging in age from 4 to 84, of whom 45% were Protestants, 36.5% Roman Catholics, 11.2% Jewish and 7.2% who are described as 'others'. The respondents were equally divided by gender but were overwhelmingly white (97.8%). On the basis of the interviews which were recorded and transcribed, Fowler and his colleagues identified six stages of faith development.

But what is the value of all this?

In a critique of faith development, Dr Sharon Parks writes

> The metaphor of *development*, dominant in Western culture and connoting movement, growth and ongoing transformation, has the power to resonate with both a deep source of traditional conviction and the sense of contemporary reality within the American (immigrant) soul. At the same time, the understanding of faith in which this theory rests, faith as a broad human phenomenon not exclusively bound by cultic religious control, both opens up the religious imagination and serves as a solvent of the secular resistance to religion. In short, faith development theory offers a dynamic language for an understanding of faith and religion that provides one way of addressing the reality of change and pluralism in a secular world. Yet its concern for the quality of mature faith counters the conventional dogma of relativism to which an ideology of pluralism is all too vulnerable, and thus it has the power to appeal to the religious-theological mind seeking integrity within pluralism.[2]

Three of Fowler's stages of faith development take us from childhood to adulthood. As far as Merton is concerned, we have his autobiographical account of his unusual childhood and struggle to adulthood as well as his mother Ruth's diary of her son, Tom.

Intuitive-Projective Faith

Fowler's first stage of faith development he calls Intuitive-Projective Faith. It is the faith that a child develops as he or she brings together the teachings and examples of significant adults on the one hand, and his or her own cognitive egocentricity and imaginative capacity on the other. This is the stage where imagination and fantasy are unrestrained by logic, so an ageless Father Christmas (Santa Claus) can carry out an impossible mission every Christmas Eve. But there is also the danger of developing overwhelmingly terrifying or destructive images and the temptation of parents to exploit such images to encourage or compel moral or doctrinal conformity. Ruth Merton herself had read books on child psychology and noted her son's development and how he was more interested in books than toys and would pretend that he could read, and she noted he observed the natural world about him and the colour in his father's paintings. The influence of his parents and Merton's own growing imagination reflect Fowler's first stage of faith.

Mythical-Literal Faith

The second stage of faith, Fowler calls the Mythical-Literal Faith. This stage is usually reached about the age of seven when the Oedipal conflict has been resolved, and when children have the ability to think more logically and to assimilate their community's tradition. The fluid, image-centred faith of the first stage develops into new ways of finding coherence and meaning, particularly in the form of narrative and so, story, myth and drama become ways of conserving, communicating and experiencing meaning.

How Merton resolved the Oedipal conflict and how this might have affected his later relationships with women can only be a matter of speculation. His mother was dying when he was six years old and he and his brother John Paul were sent to their grandparents, (that is when they were not with their father), and this period in Merton's life was marked with the loss of his mother and his roots and education. By the age of eight, he was back with his grandparents in Douglaston and was introduced to the world of story, myth and drama. He saw movies and his grandfather's firm published comic books and children's adventure stories. Here he also assimilated the community's tradition, or rather the anti-Catholic prejudice of the household. Then at the age of nine, his father took him to another community to live in France where he was to absorb his father's artistic and religious sensitivity.

If Fowler is right and the second stage of faith development happens at about seven years of age and involves more logical thought and the discovery of story and myth and assimilation of the community's tradition then it is easy to identify this stage in Merton's childhood.

Synthetic–Conventional Faith

Around the age of twelve, Fowler sees his Stage 3 developing. He calls it Synthetic-Conventional Faith. The world of experience is becoming more complex and the youth struggles to make sense of it. The complexity makes young people look for security and adopt the opinions and authority of others. It is the conformist stage where the ability to reflect and judge and choose has not fully developed. But it is the stage when the youth develops a greater capacity for story-telling which shapes the personal myth, that is the youth can see new meanings in his or her past, and look to the future and see possible relationships and life developments. It is, however, a vulnerable stage in adolescent development and Fowler suggests that too much internalising at this stage, and too much pressure from others' expectations and judgements, can harm later autonomy or lead to despair.

During this time, when Fowler would expect an adolescent to reach Stage 3, Merton was first at the Lycée in France, which he hated but where his story-telling ability had clearly developed, because he managed to write two novels and another which he did not complete. If Stage 3 is the conformist stage, it would appear that Merton did not fit this stage of his development because he did not conform and that may well have led to his unhappiness. He was not French, he was not a Catholic and as an 'outsider' he was bullied; so when his father decided to move to England Merton was delighted and his school days in Surrey and at Oakham began.

Then at the age of 14, his father was very ill and Tom had to spend time with his father's friends in Scotland. The two girls in the household were besotted with horses, for which he did not share their enthusiasm; Tom again found himself not conforming and spending time reading alone. Life was not much brighter at Oakham. His father was dying and he was more intelligent and had a much wider experience of life and greater sophistication than the other boys. Again, he faced bullying but became captain of boxing and played rugby, so he was no weakling either physically or intellectually.

His father's death, his time at Oakham, Tom Bennett's guardianship and the time he spent in London, exposed him to the British way of life with the pre-war values typified by the Empire, Anglicanism, English literature and the English class system.

The loss of his father in adolescence must have had a profound and lasting effect on Merton. When you have lost both parents, when you feel you don't even have a country to which you belong, the crisis of self-identity and the need for love to give self-worth must have been great. Fowler's theory that interpersonal betrayal (which is one aspect of bereavement) may result in despair about an ultimate personal reality or exclusionary preoccupation with it, may be seen to explain Merton's later preoccupation(and sometimes despair) with the search for ultimate reality and self-identity of what it means to be human.

In *The Seven Storey Mountain*, Merton reflects on his childhood and adolescence to give meaning to those things that seemed to have had no meaning and he acknowledges past feelings and hurts. Merton recalls memories from his early childhood and his unhappiness at school in France. Some of what he writes will strike chords with his readers because they too will have pre-school and school memories, but for those who had less traumatic childhoods, they are likely to be limited to general impressions and particular instances. It is when Merton describes what Fowler would identify as Stage 3 in faith development that most of his readers will be readily able to identify. The impression (or lack of it) made upon him by the French Protestant pastor at the Lycée and the Anglican chaplain at Oakham, will evoke our own early impressions of clergy. Children learn prejudice, and the French Catholic attitude towards Protestants and the American Protestant attitude towards Catholics were noted by Merton and probably lurk somewhere in our own unconscious minds. Like Merton, with the benefit of hindsight we see how our adolescent years shaped the future. We may have wished it had been different, but it is part of us, and most of us reading Merton's growing-up years will be able to relate to parts of it, even if we had it somewhat easier.

Psychologists recognise that the way in which we respond to a crisis will be significant in our faith development and how we respond to a crisis will vary as to which stage we have reached. Fowler, for example, points out that a crisis in intimacy will be experienced differently by someone in Stage 2 who has not yet developed the capacity for mutual perspective taking, in comparison to people in Stages 3 or 4.[3]

Merton's moving words of an incident in Italy point to a moment of growth in faith development

> I was in my room. It was night. The light was on. Suddenly it seemed to me that Father, who had now been dead more than a year, was there with me. The sense of his presence was as vivid and as real and as startling as if he had touched my arm or spoken to me. The whole thing passed in a flash, but in that flash, instantly I was overwhelmed with a sudden and profound insight into the mystery and corruption of my own soul, and I was pierced deeply with a light that made me realise something of the condition I was in, and I was filled with horror at what I saw, and my whole being rose up in revolt against what was within me and my soul desired escape and liberation and freedom from all this with an intensity and urgency unlike anything I had ever known before. And now I think for the first time in my whole life I really began to pray...praying out of the very roots of my life and of my being, and praying to the God I had never known, to reach down towards me out of His darkness... There were a lot of tears connected with this and they did me good.[4]

This experience and his time in Cambridge indicates that Merton had moved beyond Stage 3 in which many adults appear to remain, to what Fowler described as Stage 4, Individuative-Reflective Faith.

Individuative-Reflective Faith

This is the stage faced by many undergraduates when study compels them to reflect on the origins and relativity of their beliefs and values. I can remember in my own undergraduate days the trauma faced by some theological students when faced with biblical criticism. They felt their world, everything on which they had based their beliefs and values, was collapsing under them. William Perry[5] in his study of intellectual and ethical development among college students says that the full realisation of relativism represents a drastic revolution that is emancipating for many, yet deeply disturbing for others. Infrequently, when relativism proves to be intolerable, the person will retreat into an authority-orientated dualistic structure of right and wrong.

In Fowler's theory, essential aspects mark Stage 4. Firstly, people recognise the relativity of their inherited world-view and abandon reliance on external authority thus developing their *executive ego*, which enables them to make choices, judgements, priorities and commitment, which can shape their future. Secondly, this critical questioning can lead to abandoning religious or moral landmarks resulting in a sense of loss and even of guilt. Fowler says that this demythologising has a positive side, which includes the clarifying and communication of meaning. The strength of Stage 4 enables us to reflect critically on personal identity and ideology; the weakness is that we might put too much confidence in our powers of reflection and attempt to assimilate other people's perspectives and even reality itself, into our own limited world-view. Some people will spend the greater part, if not all their lives in Stage 4 but the point about faith development theory is that faith can change, develop and be transformed and still retain its integrity.

There will be some of us who have naturally inherited the religious tradition, beliefs and commitment of our parents whilst others will have had a journey which is vastly different from the rest of their family. That is not to say that we have not all been through a growth process which made us question and examine our inherited faith systems and gone through a process of demythologising which may result in appropriating our inherited faith, disowning it or choosing another to make our own.

Following Fowler's scheme, it would appear that Merton spent the next stage of his life passing through the Individuative-Reflective Faith Stage during which he kicked over the traces at Cambridge, settled at Columbia University, faced the death of his grandparents and an emotional collapse and, to quote Monica Furlong, 'Unconsciously or half-consciously, he was seeking a solution for the dizzying emptiness of life'.[6] It was at Columbia that Merton read *The Spirit of Medieval Philosophy* by Etienne Gilson, which challenged his Protestant understanding of Catholicism. He was captured by the idea of *aseitas* and wrote

> In this one word, which can be applied to God alone, and which expresses His most characteristic attribute, I discovered an entirely new concept of God—a concept which showed me at once that the belief of Catholics was by no means the vague and rather superstitious hangover from an unscientific age that I had believed it to be.[7]

At Columbia, fellow students and both Jews, Robert Lax and Seymour Freedgood and a Hindu monk called Mahanambrata Bramachari and others encouraged Merton to explore the religious quest through the world of scholarship, art and literature which he was able to do in part through his Master's dissertation looking at St Thomas Aquinas and William Blake. There was an inner conflict within Merton of wanting the spiritual life but living a life of free morality with women, alcohol, heavy smoking and an undisciplined life style. His own private world was in chaos and the world about him was also in chaos, and facing war. That was when he made the decision to become a Catholic. At last Merton felt he belonged somewhere.

It would be possible to see Merton as one of the students to which William Perry refers as finding relativism intolerable and retreating into an authority orientated dualistic structure of right and wrong, for certainly the Catholic church in 1938 knew herself to be the one true church outside of which there was no salvation. Whilst Perry's observation might contain some element of truth in Merton's case, it would be to ignore the grace at work in Merton's spiritual quest and his intellectual integrity and independence of mind, which he was to demonstrate later.

The next period in Merton's life was focused on testing his vocation. Rejection by the Franciscans was later followed by acceptance by the Cistercians and monastic formation and studies for the priesthood. Cistercian life at Gethsemani was austere but Merton embraced it and wrote about it partly in his autobiography and also in his book *The Silent Life* with its apophatic, life-denying emphasis. Merton's happiness in his life of penance and his triumphalistic account of his ordination to the priesthood combined with the outstanding and unexpected success of *The Seven Storey Mountain* gave the impression of someone who had found himself, arrived and was at peace in the pre-Vatican II monastic life. Reflecting on his autobiography twenty years later, he wrote

> Perhaps if I were to attempt this book today, it would be written differently. Who knows? But it was written when I was still young and that is the way it remains. The story no longer belongs to me, and I have no right to tell it in a different way, or to imagine that it should have been seen through wiser eyes. In its present form, which will remain its only form, it belongs to many people. The author no longer has an exclusive claim upon his story. [8]

Merton had moved on in his faith journey and indeed it would seem that his divine discontent was there even before his solemn profession. He wrote

> By the time I made my vows, I decided that I was no longer sure what a contemplative was, or what the contemplative vocation was or what my vocation was, and what our Cistercian vocation was. In fact I could not be sure I knew or understood much of anything except that I believed that You wanted me to take those particular vows in this particular house on that particular day for reasons best known to Yourself, and that what I was expected to do after that was follow along with the rest and do what I was told and things would begin to come clear.[9]

Things were indeed to become clearer as Merton's questioning and prayer led him to that stage of faith development which Fowler describes as Stage 5—Conjunctive Faith.

Conjunctive Faith

The move to Stage 5 comes about with the realisation that life is not adequately comprehended by the clarifications and abstractions which have previously supported the life of faith. There is an awakening of a sense of the deeper possibilities within oneself and the symbols and paradoxes of our religious tradition insistently challenge the neatness of our Stage 4 faith. It is called conjunctive faith because it recognises that people can face the paradoxes and contradiction in themselves and in their experiences but also attain some measure of integration.

Stage 5 is reached with the realisation that we live in a relativistic world and those who reach this stage of faith are genuinely open to the truths of other communities and traditions and with humility recognise that ultimate truth extends far beyond the reach of every tradition, including his or her own. As Fowler put it, conjunctive faith, 'combines loyalty to one's primary communities of value and belief with loyalty to the reality of a community of communities.'[10]

Christians are divided in their approach to relativism. If relativism is defined as a theory that absolute truth, certainty or standards of judgement cannot be reached, then fundamentalist Christians will violently disagree, saying that the absolute truth is revealed in the Bible. Conservative Catholics might also argue that absolute truth is found in the teachings of the Church. Others will claim that Jesus is himself the truth but that from this side of the grave we can only 'see through a glass darkly', wrestle with the truth as found in scripture and tradition and see Jesus as the ultimate and fullest revelation of God. That, however, is not to say that God's truth is not found elsewhere in other cultures and faith communities and expressed in ways that may be new and refreshing.

One of the lessons that Merton learned when he entered Gethsemani was that whilst he was surrounded by Cistercian faith and liturgical and other practices and caught up in its high ideals, he was still the same person and still had a need to express himself in writing. 'Conversion of manners' was to be a life work and not an instant transformation, but he nevertheless became aware of the deeper possibilities within himself. In his writings we see a questioning of the Cistercian monastic life and what it means to be a contemplative, and this led to his request to explore his vocation with the Carthusians or Camaldolese. We also see in Merton a growth from being world-denying and despising all the pleasures outside the monastery to a life-embracing approach. Whilst he always recognised the false values of society, he began to experience a deep love for people. His experience on the corner of Fourth and Walnut Streets is often seen as Merton's moment of disclosure.

> In Louisville, at the corner of Fourth and Walnut, in the centre of the shopping district, I was suddenly overwhelmed with the realisation that I loved all those people, that they were mine and I theirs, that we could not be alien to one another even though we were total strangers... Then it was as though I suddenly saw the secret beauty of their hearts, the depths of their hearts where neither sin nor desire nor self-knowledge can reach, the core of their reality, the person that each one is in God's eyes. If only they could see themselves as they really are.[11]

Paradoxically, Merton's deeply felt love for people was expressed in his desire to be apart from them because he recognised that so often in spiritual terms, to be on the edge is in reality to be at the centre. Gilbert Shaw, an Anglican priest expressed it in these terms.

> Withdrawal does not deprive the solitary of his humanity and all that that implies in terms of his relationship, for his coinherence in mankind is by his natural birth... For him, withdrawal emphasises the fact of his relationship with man, because through the deepening of

his prayer in solitude he comes to a deeper realisation of his coinherence with mankind.[12]

But for Merton, withdrawal was not only to achieve a greater unity with people in prayer but also to be a powerful symbol of humanity's true values. He wrote in *Contemplation in a World of Action*:

> Whereas in the fourth century monks were determined to prove their solitude characteristic by showing it to be beyond the human, the situation today is quite the reverse... The hermit exists today to realise and experience in himself the ordinary values of a life lived with the minimum of artificiality. Such a life will, from the beginning, seem itself artificial because it is so completely unlike the lives of other people.[13]

Conjunctive faith, according to Fowler, is when paradoxes and contradictions can be faced whilst still attaining a degree of integration, so for Merton there appears to be no conflict between embracing the world and choosing the hermit life. Again, Merton demonstrates his ability to face paradox and contradiction in his ecumenical outreach. During his life understanding of what it means to be a Catholic – of belonging to a Church with its buildings, priesthood, the Mass, monastic life and hierarchy – had broadened and when he wrote of his conversion to Catholicism, as a son of St Benedict, he preferred to speak of his conversion to Christ. Merton's understanding of Catholicism and the Church was of the world in the process of redemption. He wrote

> For me, Catholicism is not confined to one culture, one nation, one age, and one race. My faith is not a mixture of the Irish Catholicism of the United States and the splendid and vital Catholicism reborn during the last war, of my native France... My Catholicism is all the world and in all ages. It dates from the beginning of the world.[14]

Merton went on to speak of the Church of the future with an appropriate message for us today:

> For many in our New World, the Church is merely a respectable institution closely linked to a past society. This is a grave mistake and a disastrous error—an error that we clergy and religious must try to dissipate, not only with our teaching but also with our lives. We love our old traditions but we are men of the future. Our responsibility is to the future, not the past. The past does not depend on us, the future does.[15]

Brother Patrick Hart describes Merton's spirit of ecumenism as a natural consequence of his monastic and contemplative experience and that in its renewal the monastic life must preserve or acquire an ecumenical relevance in the form of an openness to discuss our differences.

> Merton saw clearly the unique dimension that the monastic life could contribute to ecumenical experience by deepening the unity that comes about not only by dialogue with our separated brethren, but above all by being silent with them, and sharing our solitude with them. A contemplative monastery should provide this kind of atmosphere or climate for mutual fraternal exchange and prayer.[16]

Merton was in the forefront of encouraging ecumenical encounter at Gethsemani even before Vatican II. In the fifties, groups of Episcopalian, Methodist, Baptist and Disciples of Christ seminarians or exchange students came to experience life at the Abbey and to engage with Merton and some of his fellow monks in ecumenical dialogue. Throughout the fifties and sixties his correspondence and journals reveal an ecumenical approach which goes well beyond welcoming home the separated brethren or resolving theological disagreements. It displays a post-critical attitude of discovering unity in oneself which is characteristic of Fowler's description of Conjunctive faith.

> If I can unite in myself the thought and the devotion of Eastern and Western Christendom, the Greek and the Latin Fathers, the Russian with the Spanish mystics, I can prepare in myself the reunion of divided Christians. From that secret and unspoken unity in myself can eventually come a visible and manifest unity of all Christians. If we want to bring together what is divided, we can not do so by imposing one division upon the other or absorbing one division into the other. But if we do this, the union is not Christian. It is political, and doomed to further conflict. We must contain all divided worlds in ourselves and transcend them in Christ.[17]

Fowler says that conjunctive faith combines loyalty to one's own primary communities of value and belief with loyalty to the reality of a 'community of communities' and this Merton clearly did in his commitment to solitude and the world and his commitment to the Roman Catholic Church and other Christians, but Fowler goes on to warn that the emergent strength of the Conjunctive Faith stage is the *ironic imagination*, the capacity to become powerfully engaged by symbolic expressions, even while recognising their relativity and ultimate inadequacy for representing transcendent reality. The danger here is becoming paralysed by the irresolvable paradoxes and polarities, a state of disunity that can lead to a sense of 'cosmic homelessness and loneliness'.

I suppose it is legitimate to ask if Merton experienced that state of cosmic homelessness and loneliness. His ecumenical involvement seemed to naturally open up the question of interfaith relations and a deeper and wider search for an understanding of truth and contemplation. Did he still belong in the confines of a Cistercian Abbey or had his spiritual horizons made him equally at home in the Himalayas? Although surrounded by friends, admirers and spiritual children, was Merton a lonely man who perhaps felt more at home with his Zen Buddhist monk friends than with some of his own Cistercian brethren?

Towards the end of his life, two particular areas of concern link with Fowler's Stage 6, which he calls Universalising Faith—that is Merton's passion for peace and justice issues and for interfaith relations.

Universalising Faith

This sixth stage of faith development has been the one most questioned by Fowler's critics. I should also add that Fowler doesn't suggest that people suddenly move from one stage of development to another but that there is a gradual growth and progression. Indeed, in his own research, when trying to place people at different stages of faith development, he uses eleven stages because he places many people as being between two stages.

In recognising the discomfort of Stage 5 with its irresolvable paradoxes and polarities, a state of disunity which can lead to a sense of 'cosmic homelessness and loneliness', Fowler sees certain rare individuals as being called into a new, transformed relation to the ultimate environment which he calls universalising faith. This leads to a *decentration of faith*, in which they embrace the knowing and valuing of the world as experienced by others which then leads to the *emptying of self* through detachment. Controversially, Fowler cites Gandhi, Mother Teresa of Calcutta and Martin Luther King Jr as examples of people who have reached this stage. Fowler is not, however, saying that they have achieved perfection but rather, that although still limited and blinded in certain respects, these exceptional people, through their struggles with various difficulties, have become selfless proponents of a redeemed world.

The sign of having reached Stage 6 is the ability for people to embrace the world as their community and demonstrate an all-consuming commitment to peace and justice. The monastic life has traditionally taught the need for humility and self-emptying in imitation of the kenosis of Christ who emptied himself at the incarnation. Merton also understood the importance of this:

> But if the Truth is to make me free, I must let go my hold upon myself, and not retain the semblance of a self which is an object or a 'thing'. I too must be no-thing. And when I am no-thing, I am in the All, and Christ lives in me. But He who lives in me is in all those around me. He who lives in the chaotic world of men is hidden in the midst of them, unknowable and unrecognisable because he is no-thing. Thus in the cataclysms of our world, with its crimes, its lies and its fantastic violence, He who suffers in all is the All who still cannot suffer. Yet in us, it is He who suffers, that we may live in Him.[18]

By the 1960s Merton's outlook moved from the apophatic life-denying and world hating monk of his autobiography to the kataphatic life-embracing monk who "chose the world" and could write

> To choose the world is to choose to do the work I am capable of doing, in collaboration with my brothers, to make the world better, more free, more just, more liveable, more human. Rejection of the world and 'contempt for the world' is in fact not a choice but the evasion of choice.[19]

Merton, the "guilty bystander" saw the need to speak out for the voiceless and oppressed and challenge those who colluded with racism or war. He was among the first Catholics to condemn any use of nuclear weapons, although his superiors tried to silence him at first. Merton believed that war was outside the kingdom of God and not a fit activity for Christians. Drawing on the scriptures, the writings of the Fathers and his own critique of St Augustine and the Just War theory, Merton engaged with others in expressing his opposition to war and the use of weapons of mass destruction. He was unequivocal in his condemnation of the Vietnam War and like Gandhi was a proponent of non-violent resistance.

His opponents, of course, pointed out that nuclear weapons could not be un-invented and that whilst contemplation may help to provide depth and perspective to life, it did not solve the problem faced by world leaders. Merton was not suggesting that it did but he provided a prophetic voice which showed the danger of power, the futility of the Vietnam war, the move away from Christian moral principles, the need to form a conscience and for peace-building.

Merton had also experienced a radical change in outlook when it came to interfaith interests and in particular with his growing interest in eastern religions. In 1948, he wrote

> Ultimately, I suppose all Oriental mysticism can be reduced to techniques that do the same thing (i.e. achieve relaxation), but in a far more subtle and advanced fashion: and if that is true, it is not mysticism at all. It remains purely in the natural order. That does not make it evil per se, according to Christian standards: but it does not make it good, in relation to the supernatural. It is simply more or less useless, except when it is mixed up with elements that are strictly diabolical: and then of course these dreams and annihilations are designed to wipe out all vital moral activity, while leaving the personality in control of some nefarious principle, either of his own, or from outside himself.[20]

Ten years after dismissing Oriental mysticism as little more than a relaxation technique, we see Merton sharing his manuscript, The Wisdom of the Desert with Dr Suzuki, a teacher of Zen. From 1961, Merton spent much time in the systematic study of Asian religions and philosophies helped by his Chinese friend Professor Wu who was a convert to Catholicism, but who had brought his own understanding of Zen, Taoism and Confucianism into Christianity. Merton was convinced that Asian wisdom could enrich Western Christianity. He agreed with the 16th century Jesuits that Confucianism should be viewed as a 'sacred philosophy' similar to Christianity and that both had an answer for the problem of alienation. But it was Taoism in which Merton found a greater similarity with Christianity and in particular the works of a recluse called Chuang Tzu, and when he wrote his The Way of Chuang Tzu in 1965 he indicated that he had enjoyed writing this book "more than any other I can remember".[21] Merton was particularly attracted to Taoism's teaching about the complementarity of opposites with which he could identify in his own life and which Fowler associates with Conjunctive faith.

It was, however, Zen Buddhism that most attracted Merton because he saw it having the potential for world peace, finding meaning in ordinary life, bringing together heart and mind and finding self-knowledge and transcendence. He wrote in *Zen and the Birds of Appetite*

> I believe that Zen has much to say not only to a Christian but also to a modern man. It is non-doctrinal, concrete, direct, and existential and seeks above all to come to grips with life itself, not with ideas about life.[22]

Nevertheless, Merton saw the similarities between Christianity and Buddhism with meditation as a way to approach suffering and achieving peace and harmony but he also recognised the differences. Realising that discussions about doctrine were fruitless, Merton engaged with his Eastern friends on the basis of religious experience and ultimate goals.

Merton had also encountered Hinduism through Dr Brahmachari in his Columbia student days and in later studies of yoga, but he nevertheless found it too speculative. He also found that some of the battle accounts in the *Bhagavad Gita* clashed with his pacifism. On the other hand, he was able to identify with the fusion of action, worship and contemplation of Hinduism and acknowledge

> Since it is perfectly obvious that a Sadhu might well know God better and love Him better than a lukewarm Christian, I see no problem whatsoever about declaring that such a one is closer to Him and is even, by that fact, closer to Christ. [23]

Merton's love for Asia – its philosophy, mysticism and religion – made him long to visit the continent. His abbot, Dom James Fox, thwarted one opportunity, but in 1968 his dream came true. There was a new abbot and he agreed that Merton could be a speaker at a Benedictine conference in Bangkok. He was able to combine his visit with visits to Christian and Buddhist monasteries in various countries and Merton kept a journal of his visit, a visit from which only his body was to return—in the hold of a US plane, ironically also carrying the bodies of soldiers who had died in Vietnam.

During his Asian visit, he stayed at Dharamsala, the home of the Dalai Lama. There he had a dream that he was back in Gethsemani in the habit of a Buddhist monk. Perhaps that expresses something of his identification with the East or his concern as to how he would take his Asian experience back with him to Gethsemani.

Fowler believed that those who attain Stage 6 embrace the world as their community and demonstrate an all-consuming commitment to justice and love. Merton would certainly seem to fit his definition.

Conclusion

What James Fowler has done is to suggest that there are indeed stages of faith which are common to us all. Psychology of religion is not an exact science and others have criticised Fowler's approach or produced theories of their own including Meissner, a Jesuit psychoanalyst whose own scheme identifies five modes of religious experience; but even Meissner himself wrote, 'Fowler's work represents a fundamental contribution to our understanding of the human experience of faith'.[24] Fowler, I believe, enables us to take a fresh look at how faith develops within us and to discern Merton's own faith development. This in turn enables us to see our own journey more clearly and to journey with others through their stages of faith.

I began by suggesting that Merton's story is our story because his faith journey will in some way parallel our own faith journey. Although Merton's life is likely to have been very different from our own, yet he is not a stranger to us nor did he find others strangers to him. Whether standing on the corner of Fourth and Walnut Avenues, or in a Hindu Ashram or Buddhist monastery, he was not among strangers but with fellow pilgrims like us, who are also at some stage on our personal faith journey.

Notes and References

1. *Thomas Merton in France*, Simon Fraser University leaflet, 1999
2. Sharon Parks, *The North American Critique of James Fowler's Theory of Faith Deveopment* in Stages of Faith and Religious Development (SCM Press, 1989), p.103
3. James Fowler, *Stages of Faith: The Psychology of Human Development and the Quest for Meaning* (San Francisco: Harper & Row, 1981), p.107
4. Thomas Merton, *Elected Silence*, (London: Burns & Oates, 1961), p.84
5. William Perry, *Forms of Intellectual and Ethical Development in the College Years* (New York: Holt, Rinehart & Winston, 1970)
6. Monica Furlong, *Merton: A Biography*, (London: SPCK, 1995), p.66
7. Thomas Merton, *Elected Silence* op.cit. p.114

8. Thomas Merton, *Reflections on my Work*, (London: Fount Paperbacks,1981), p.71

9. Thomas Merton, *Elected Silence*, op.cit. p.298

10. James Fowler, *Becoming Adult, Becoming Christian: Adult Development and Christian Faith*, (San Francisco: Harper & Row, 1984), p.67

11. Thomas Merton: *Conjectures of a Guilty Bystander*, (New York: Doubleday, 1966), p.141-2

12. Gilbert Shaw, *The Christian Solitary*, (Oxford: SLG Press, 1969) p.7

13. Thomas Merton, *Contemplation in a World of Action*, (New York: Doubleday, 1971), p.166

14. Thomas Merton, *Reflections on my Work*, op.cit. p.50

15. Thomas Merton, Ibid. p.51

16. Patrick Hart OCSO, *Thomas Merton, Monk: A Monastic Tribute* (London: The Catholic Bookclub 1976) p.210

17. Thomas Merton, *Conjectures of a Guilty Bystander*, op. cit. p.12

18. Thomas Merton, *The Seven Storey Mountain* (New York: Harcourt Brace & Co., 1948) preface

19. Thomas Merton, *Is the World a Problem?* (Commonweal 84)

20. Thomas Merton, *Elected Silence*, op.cit.

21. Thomas Merton, *The Way of Chuang Tzu*, New York: New Directions, 1965) p.9, 10

22. Thomas Merton, *Zen and the Birds of Appetite*, (New York: New Directions, 1968) p.32

23. Thomas Merton, *Letter to Philip Griggs (Swami Yogeshanada)* Unpublished, 22 June, 1965

24. W. W. Meissner, SJ, *Psychoanalysis and Religious Experience*, (New Haven, Conn: Yale University Press, 1987) p.136

THOMAS MERTON
a mind awake in the dark

THE POETRY OF THOMAS MERTON

Five of Merton's poems,
presented with a commentary

Mosaic: St Praxed's

DAVID SCOTT

Mosaic: St Praxed's

So like a quiet pigeon in a hollowed rock
You stand there in the wall's curve
Made of stone needled tapestry
In this dim sheltered paradise
Mary made of love art and poetry

In the obscure and flaming chapel
Where gold and ruby hold the azure
Conch of sweetly burning peace
You welcome me refuge pure
To see you O soul's delight

Deeply forgetful of the evil by our side
We sail above our strange agony
Chained utterly Mary to your joy

February 1933

MERTON SETS OFF for an extended holiday in Italy. A serious illness, his place at Cambridge, a camping holiday in the New Forest, and a Bournemouth Hotel romance had been put behind him. He arrived in Rome. The 17 year old Merton began to feel a pulse in his soul and a longing to pray. It was not the usual sights that moved him, neither the "vapid, boring, semi-pornographic statuary of the Empire" nor the ecclesiastical monuments of the Renaissance and Counter-Reformation that he had first sought out as a dutiful tourist reading his Baedeker. Rather, it was the city's most ancient churches. In particular, for our purposes, the church of St Praxed's. Here and in other churches, he discovered 'the Christ of the Byzantine icons'. In his autobiography, Merton writes:

> And now for the first time in my life I began to find out something of Who this Person was that men called Christ. It was obscure, but it was a true knowledge of Him, in some sense, truer than I knew and truer than I would admit. But it was in Rome that my conception of Christ was formed. It was there I first saw Him, Whom I now serve as my God and my King, and Who owns and rules my life. (*The Seven Storey Mountain*, Harcourt, Brace and Company, 1948, p.109).

In practice, D. H. Lawrence was put aside, and the Gospels were taken up.

St Praxed

St Praxed was a female saint, the daughter of Pudens, a Roman senator, and his wife Servilia. St Paul the apostle is said to have lodged in the house of Pudens, and to have used it as a church. St Praxed is said to have ministered to the martyrs in prison, and to have been diligent in collecting their relics. In the nave of the church is a well, in which it is pretended the Saint cast the sponge wherewith she had sopped up the blood of many martyrs. Her relics are preserved in the church. She is represented in art with a basin in one hand and a bunch of palms in the other, though she did not herself suffer martyrdom.

Columbia University and Jacques Maritain

The next piece of the mosaic of this poem begins in 1935 when Merton was at Columbia University. He heard, under Mark Van Doren's tutorship, of a modern scholastic called Jacques Maritain. Here was someone who could encourage Merton in his interest in the connections between Catholicism and the world of culture. At Columbia he found others who shared his passions.

> They stand in the stacks of libraries and turn over pages of St Thomas's *Summa* with a kind of curious reverence. They talk in seminars about "Thomas" and "Scotus" and "Augustine" and "Bonaventure" and they are familiar with Maritain and Gilson, and they have read all the poems of Hopkins—and indeed they know more about what is best in Catholic literary and philosophical tradition than most Catholics ever do on this earth. (SSM, p.175).

Maritain helped Merton through the difficulties and contradictions that he felt between sociology and economics on the one hand, and faith and charity on the other, in his thesis on the poems of Blake. Merton met Jacques Maritain through Dan Walsh who had been a student and collaborator of Gilson and knew Maritain well. Merton was introduced to Maritain at the Catholic Book Club, "where this most saintly philosopher had been giving a talk on Catholic Action". (SSM, p.219) No mention yet of Jacques's wife, Raïssa, although she too had been among the library stacks. Raïssa is the author of the poem, 'Mosaic: St Praxed's'.

Raïssa Oumancoff (1883-1960)

Raïssa was a Russian Jewish emigrée and a student at the Sorbonne where she met her future husband Jacques Maritain. They met in 1900, and were married four years later. In 1906, together with Raïssa's sister, Vera, they were baptized in the Roman Catholic Church; Léon Bloy was their godfather. Raïssa shared Jacques' intellectual interests, and as philosophers, poets and social critics, and above all as contemplatives, they made their mark on twentieth century catholicism. With Merton, they shared a commitment to art, wisdom, and social action. Like Merton they recognised contemplation, or as Raïssa called it, 'receuillement', as the source from which all else flowed. Jacques and Raïssa lived in the United States for a time during World War II, and again from 1948-1960, while Jacques taught at Princeton. They returned to France shortly before Raïssa's death in November 1960. She was buried at Kolbsheim, Alsace and in 1973 when Jacques died in Toulouse, where he lived with the Little Brothers of Jesus and had professed religious vows, he was buried in the same tomb as Raïssa.

Une à Une

Raïssa Maritain shines out of Merton's work in brief shafts of light. They were soul to soul. As Raïssa said, and Merton put as a quotation at the front of *Emblems of a Season of Fury*:

> Et il n'y aura pas d'acquittement pour les nations
> Mais seulement pour les âmes une à une.
> (We shall never have an acquittal for the nations
> But only for souls one to one)

For our purposes here, the significant joining of souls, came with Merton's translation of six poems and a prose piece of Raïssa's, which were published in Emblems of a Season of Fury, among which was 'Mosaic: St Praxed's'. Emblems came out from New Directions in 1963. Merton wrote to James Laughlin,

> I have done some new translations, this time from Raïssa Maritain... who was a remarkable person. Her poems are very individual and reflect a deep and simple personality that is most impressive. Probably won't be wildly popular with some people, but I think they have, as the blurbs say, "lasting significance" (TM to JL, Jan 11,1963).

Raïssa's Journal

After Raïssa's death, Jacques sent Merton a signed copy of Raïssa's Journal. Merton's letter to Jacques, (Dec.18, 1962) thanking him for sending the book is very revealing of how Merton thought of Raïssa, and her writings:

> The document is like a sunrise, a wonder that is ordinary but if you are more attentive you find it an outstanding event. I read it in solitude in the woods. Each sentence opens our heart to God. It's a book full of windows. What moves me most is that in each line I see and I hear this "child" of Proverbs 8.27-31 "ludens in orbe terrarum" (playing over his whole world), ludens too in Raïssa. I dreamed a few times of this child (who for the first time presented herself as a girl of the race of St Anne) and she was sad and quiet because everyone was making fun of her strange name which was "Proverb". Also another time on a Louisville street I saw suddenly that everyone was "Proverb", without knowing it. Raïssa's words are filled with the presence and the light of this wisdom-child. She is 'Proverb'... Especially she reminds me of that mystic that I love above all others, Julian of Norwich. (Raïssa even speaks of the maternal knees of God.) She has the same tone, the same candour.
>
> O thank you dear Jacques for this beautiful book with my name written by Raïssa's hand, on the first page. How precious this gift is to me. It will often remind me that I must be faithful to Proverb, the poor, the unknown. Pray so that I may be faithful.
>
> Some time ago I told (John Howard) Griffin...that I wanted to translate some of Raïssa's poems that do not exist in English beginning with the one about Chagall. Some others too, but I don't have them. Tell me who the publishers are and if you will allow me to translate and publish them, not all but about a dozen. (Letter, Dec 18, 1962, The Courage for Truth, pp.33,34)

Raïssa's Notes sur le Pater

In 1962 Raïssa's Notes on the Lord's Prayer (Notes sur le Pater) was published. Merton quoted short sections from it at the end of his book, now known as The Climate of Monastic Prayer. He was finishing this essay on his Asian journey. The Managing Editor of the Cistercian Fathers Series received a note the day after Merton's death which read, "I guess I ought to read the galleys for this book but I am not sure where I'll be. Asia has been magnificent so far and more to come. Best always, Tom Merton." Raïssa is quoted on almost the last page of this book. They were almost her last printed words, and they are written in Merton's last book of printed words.

> If there were fewer wars, less thirst to dominate and to exploit others, less national egoism, less egoism of class and caste, if man were more concerned for his brother, and really wanted to collect together, for the good of the human race, all the resources which science places at his disposal especially today, there would be fewer children who die or are incurably weakened by undernourishment.

She goes on, says Merton, to ask what obstacles man has placed in the way of the Gospel that this should be so. It is unfortunately true that those who have complacently imagined themselves blessed by God have in fact done more than others to frustrate his will. But Raïssa Maritain says that perhaps the poor, who have never been able to seek the Kingdom of God, may be found by it "when they leave the world which has not recognized in them the image of God." In Conjectures (p.318) Merton mentions that he is writing a preface to Julie Kernan's translation of Raïssa's beautiful little book on the Pater.

The poem itself

So much for secondary sources. What about the poem? It's short. It's a translation from the French. It doesn't rhyme. I haven't seen the mosaic myself, and although Merton had visited St Praxed's, he might not necessarily have seen it, or remembered it, either. Raïssa, spending time while her husband worked in Rome, obviously did, and it moved her greatly. So all we have is the poem, in order to paint for ourselves the visual picture. This mosaic is of Mary, the Mother of our Lord, and it is on a part of the church which is not flat but rounded, "in the wall's curve", that's feminine for a start, and she is as if nestling like a pigeon in a hollowed rock, and so, natural, discreet, but visible. The quality of the mosaic is like a tapestry, but seems to be sewn into stone; soft, but integral with the very stone of the building. There are no punctuation marks, you will notice, in the poem, and so there are various combinations of phrases you can make. The words belong to other words with a will of their own.

The "dim sheltered paradise" takes us to the churches Merton liked in New York which were dark and numinous. Donne said, "churches are best for prayer, that have least light": and here is one of them, with in it an image of the Blessed Virgin, whose constituent parts are not earth, air, fire and water, but love, art and poetry. Then come the visual fireworks:

> the flaming chapel
> Where gold and ruby hold the azure
> Conch ...

'Conch' is a strange word, it reminds me of Golding's Lord of the Flies, and the conch which was used to call a meeting, but probably here it is meant in its architectural meaning "domed roof of semi-circular apse".

> You welcome me refuge pure
> To see you O soul's delight.

This is 'Love bade me welcome', and 'God is my refuge and my strength', and the Song of Songs 7: 6, 'How fair and how pleasant art thou, O love, for delights.'

> You welcome me refuge pure
> To see you O soul's delight

And then, Raïssa is:

> Deeply forgetful of the evil by our side

Conscious of the evil, but freed from its chains, we are chained only to the joy which captures us in Mary. Finally, "we sail above our strange agony". The heights and levels of this poem are very important. I don't know, but I'm sure the mosaic is at a height, and by associating with the Virgin we too are aloft. We are sailing along, like Mary on the heights of Judah, urgent to see Elizabeth to share the news, described in one of Merton's most memorable images, in his poem 'The Quickening of John the Baptist':

> Why are your clothes like sails?

We are sailing to heaven, well above "our strange agony", whatever that might be for us. "Strange" because agony is foreign to our true nature. The nature to which Mary gave birth should not be strange to us, as humans, for in Christ we share his humanity. Agony, even if it is a stage on the journey, is not our final destination.

Chained utterly Mary to your joy

Now, of course, we are eager to see this mosaic with our own eyes, and yet, and yet: in a way we have seen it. Perhaps even more clearly than it may be seen in St Praxed's. We have seen it through the eyes of that difficult to translate French word, 'receuillement'. Does it mean meditation, or is it more than that, the process of seeing the secrets of God?

A final quote from Raïssa Maritain:

> It seems that the Holy Spirit grows in the heart 'recueilli', silent and burning with love. Profound silence is lyrical. It opens the heart in a mystical way, it experiences the whole range of humility, joy, and love, without a word being said. (*Journal*).

The heart "recueilli". This was the state of the heart of Merton in 1933 on his visit to Rome. In a letter to Jacques Maritain discussing the translation of Raïssa's writings, he wrote

> The best word for receuillement would be it seems to me, ABSORPTION (December 20, 1966, *The Courage for Truth*, p.50).

His prayer, through its attention to the word and the image, and the world around him, allowed him, as it allows us, to be absorbed into God.

For My Brother:
Reported Missing in Action, 1943

MICHAEL WOODWARD

For My Brother: Reported Missing in Action, 1943

Sweet brother, if I do not sleep
My eyes are flowers for your tomb;
And if I cannot eat my bread,
My fasts shall live like willows where you died.
If in the heat I find no water for my thirst,
My thirst shall turn to springs for you, poor traveller.

Where, in what desolate and smokey country,
Lies your poor body, lost and dead?
And in what landscape of disaster
Has your unhappy spirit lost its road?

Come, in my labor find a resting place
And in my sorrows lay your head,
Or rather take my life and blood
And buy yourself a better bed—
Or take my breath and take my death
And buy yourself a better rest.

When all the men of war are shot
And flags have fallen into dust,
Your cross and mine shall tell men still
Christ died on each, for both of us.

For in the wreckage of your April Christ lies slain,
And Christ weeps in the ruins of my spring:
The money of Whose tears shall fall
Into your weak and friendless hand,
And buy you back to your own land:

The silence of Whose tears shall fall
Like bells upon your alien tomb.
Hear them and come: they call you home.

I LIKE THIS poem. It's been good to get to know it better and study it more closely.

It stands out among the Thirty Poems in which it first appeared in 1944, stands out in the Selected Poems, and stands out as one of Merton's most fully achieved poems.

It is also distinctive for its subject matter. The dreadful hurt of losing his brother could only happen once. Merton rose to meet the brutal finality of his brother's death with a poem of weight and depth, providing a lasting memorial and a shaft of resurrection light in the darkness of his loss. In so doing he has achieved something universal about trusting God's love in the face of death. It is a poem of clear-eyed hope.

Ten minutes is a short time to spend on a poem with many layers and considerable subtlety. So I'm not going into possible sources in St Bernard or an elegy by Catullus for his own brother, and I'm not going in for a line by line commentary.

I want to simply move through the text and point up a few moments of special resonance.

But first I would like to set the poem in the context of the relationship between John Paul and his elder brother. On the whole, I'm dubious about introducing material from outside a poem. But in this case I think it enriches our reading to be reminded of the salient points.

I think it's fair to describe their early relationship as troubled. Tom understandably felt his place as le fils unique usurped, and his exclusive claim on his mother's attention diluted. Tom was three and a half when John Paul was born.

Tom wrote:

> He was a child with a much serener nature than mine...I remember that...in the long evenings when he was put to bed before the sun went down, instead of protesting or fighting, as I did when I had to go to bed, he would lie upstairs in his crib, and we would hear him singing a little tune.[1]

The contrast contributed to the young Merton's sense of himself as unworthy and unsatisfactory. In their early life the brothers were not soulmates or even playmates. With an age gap of nearly four years it's not surprising.

We have that terribly poignant image Merton wrote about in The Seven Storey Mountain:

> The picture I get of my brother John Paul is this: standing in a field, about a hundred yards away from the clump of sumachs where we have built our hut, is this little perplexed five-year old kid in short pants and a kind of leather jacket standing quite still, with his arms hanging down at his sides, and gazing in our direction, afraid to come any nearer on account of the stones, as insulted as he was saddened, and his eyes full of indignation and sorrow. And yet he does not go away. We shout at him to get out of there, to beat it, and go home, and wing a couple of more rocks in that direction, and he does not go away. We tell him to play in some other place. He does not move.[2]

After Merton's mother's death in 1921, much of their growing-up was apart: Tom away with his father or at school, John Paul with Ruth's family on Long Island. Later on, they grew closer, becoming movie addicts and going camping together. With the war and American neutrality, John Paul enlisted by crossing the border and joining the Royal Canadian Air Force in Toronto. The war brought a concentration to their relationship. John Paul spent his 1942 embarkation leave at Gethsemani. Tom saw John Paul for the first time in the uniform of Sergeant Observer. He had been trained to read aerial photographs, and distinguish what was going on on the ground (he was not a pilot as Monica Furlong's book[4] maintains). John Paul had decided to become a Catholic, and it was wisely arranged for Tom to do most of the instructing, even though he was simply a novice rather than a priest. They spent time talking among the Stations of the Cross. Before John Paul left the brothers received Holy Communion together.

Michael Mott writes:

> The Chapel of our Lady of Victories was ever after a place for Merton where a greater mystery than reconciliation had taken place. Here, finally, he had been helped to help his brother. Before they had been little more to each other than orphans of the same parents. [5]

John Paul left in July 1942 for England. By early Spring he had married a young radio operator in the A.T.S., Margaret Evans. News of this event came to Merton on Easter Monday in a letter held over for him because of Lent. The next day he was called to the Abbot to receive a telegram saying that his brother had been reported missing ten days earlier. Soon the details came though of his broken neck, his delirium during hours adrift with his crew in a rubber dinghy, calling for water; his burial at sea.

Thérèse Lentfoehr tells us that the holograph manuscript of the poem is dated April 28, the day after the telegram.[6] So Merton probably began the poem, and may even have finished it, without knowing the details of John Paul's death. I can't be as certain of this as Patrick O'Connell seems to be.[7] The poem itself, however, deals wholeheartedly with a death: there is no sense of a question mark. So the title tag "Reported Missing" takes on a special poignancy: it is, perhaps, a subliminal denial of the facts, bearing a vestigal hope that it was all a mistake.

That background gives us an insight into the weight of emotion carried by the opening "Sweet brother." It has taken death to call this "sweet" forth. It contains Tom's remorse for past hostility, regret for the words never spoken; appreciation of what he has suddenly lost; the pathos of his brother's untimely death.

Drawing on his very recent experience of Lenten fasts and the reality of manual work in the Kentucky sunshine, in the first stanza Merton weaves this stuff of his daily life into a parallel structure redolent of the psalms he was chanting by night and day in the Abbey church. His own discomfort is offered as a sacrifice, becoming "flowers", "food" and "water" to bring comfort to his brother.

What impresses throughout the poem is its sombre, restrained ritual. It needs that strong framework to contain the intensity of the emotion. The mechanical rhythm and clipped vocabulary work to the same end.

The first sentence of the second stanza deals with the pain of not knowing where his "poor" brother's body lies. Ironically, John Paul, the trained Sergeant Observer, would have been the one best equipped to find it. But it is the "unhappy spirit" of his brother, and its fate in the "landscape of disaster" that preoccupies the poet from now on.

Merton goes on to offer more than his physical discomfort. He moves from "labor", to "life" and "blood" to "breath" and "death": anything and everything to give his brother peace.

But then, in the fourth stanza, the audacity and impracticality of this rhetoric is acknowledged. The perspective of time is introduced, with the "flags...fallen into dust", as the poet accepts there is no salvation or restitution he can possibly bring to his brother alone. Indeed Tom's need is as great as John Paul's. Here, at the end of the fourth stanza, the One who can redeem is revealed, the vital third presence capable of breathing life into the touching, but one-sided and ultimately sterile, dialogue of aspirations the poem has so far been.

For the suffering that has been inflicted on John Paul and offered by the poet is not wasted. It is taken up in the transforming power of the Easter mystery. The poet and John Paul will ultimately share the same death and, in doing so, share in Christ's atonement and resurrection.

This is developed particularly well in the final stanza, alive with resonances. Now, the brothers have different faces of Christ in common. John Paul has the Christ of Calvary, "slain" (and notice the stark appropriateness of the triple-stressed, "Christ lies slain..."); Merton identifies with the Christ who actively mourns: for his friend Lazarus, for the intractable city of Jerusalem. This grief is redemptive. Helpless as his brother is now, the Christ-tears are his ransom. As the paradoxes, images and tenses leap and dart, future and present time inter-penetrate. The tears become bells, suggestive of Gethsemani's own bells, tolling to summon John Paul home. A home, ironically, was the thing both brothers lacked for many years—like Christ during his public life.

Here we connect directly with the events and liturgy of Holy Week. There is an echo of the Last Supper: the money hints at Judas, and Tom's sense of his past betrayals. But in Merton's notebook the poem appears among notes on the liturgy for Holy Saturday.[8] Deeply embedded in it all is the silent waiting of Holy Saturday, and the drama of the Harrowing of Hell. John Paul becomes one of those released by Christ's power in his descent to Hell to open its gates after his death on the Cross, and before his physical resurrection.

Look especially at the rhymes here. After the metronomic pairing of "full" with "full" and "hand" with "land", the poem ends with the deft uncertainty of an internal rhyme "tomb/home". These two, in turn, are played off against another near-rhyme, "come" which rests between them in the middle of the final line. Their discordant music denotes a painful grappling with events that eschews pat answers. The triad itself is suggestive of John Paul, Tom and Christ: John Paul, the "tomb", Merton the advocate for his brother who is crying, "come", Christ, the Alpha & Omega, their destined "home".

At its end the poem has achieved a unity of sorts, a complex unity of sorts, but it is one based on hope and things unseen, and contains the dissonance of separation.

And finally, the last line. Few last lines of poems, and very few of Merton's last lines, contain any more punctuation than a stray comma. The last line tends to come in on the surge of the tide, finishing off with a flourish. But here we have a colon. To me it's like a fulcrum, a pivot or a hinge, almost the opening of a door. It's a gateway of hope, not in a naive or sentimental way but, in its movement of return, it subtly communicates a rooted belief in the communion possible between the living and the dead, and speaks of the gathering to come, when what has been lost will be restored, and the dead will be raised to new life.

Notes and References

1. Merton, Thomas. *The Seven Storey Mountain*, Harcourt, Brace and Company, Inc., New York, 1948, p.8
2. Ibid., p.23
3. Ibid., p.355
4. Furlong, Monica. *Merton: A Biography*, London, Collins 1980, p.132
5. Mott, Michael. *The Seven Mountains of Thomas Merton*, Boston, Houghton Mifflin 1984, p.221
6. Lentfoehr, Sister Thérèse. *Words and Silence: On the Poetry of Thomas Merton*, New York: A New Directions Book, 1979, p.9
7. O'Connell, Patrick F. 'Grief Transfigured: Merton's Elegy on His Brother,' *The Merton Seasonal* 18.1 (1993): pp.10-15
8. Lentfoehr, p.9

'To Credit Marvels':
Thomas Merton's "Grace's House"

PATRICK O'BRIEN

Grace's House

On the summit: it stands on a fair summit
Prepared by winds: and solid smoke
Rolls from the chimney like a snow cloud.
Grace's house is secure.

No blade of grass is not counted,
No blade of grass forgotten on this hill.
Twelve flowers make a token garden.
There is no path to the summit—
No path drawn
To Grace's house.

All the curtains are arranged
Not for hiding but for seeing out.
In one window someone looks out and winks.
Two gnarled short
Fortified trees have knotholes
From which animals look out.
From behind a corner of Grace's house
Another creature peeks out.

Important: hidden in the foreground
Most carefully drawn
The dog smiles, his foreleg curled, his eye like an aster.
Nose and collar are made with great attention:
This dog is loved by Grace!

And there: the world!
Mailbox number 5
Is full of Valentines for Grace.
There is a name on the box, name of a family
Not yet ready to be written in language.

A spangled arrow there
Points from our Coney Island
To her green sun-hill.

Between our world and hers
Runs a sweet river:
(No, it is not the road,
It is the uncrossed crystal
Water between our ignorance and her truth.)

O paradise, O child's world!
Where all the grass lives
And all the animals are aware!
The huge sun, bigger than the house
Stands and streams with life in the east
While in the west a thunder cloud
Moves away forever.
No blade of grass is not blessed
On this archetypal hill,
This womb of mysteries.

I must not omit to mention a rabbit
And two birds, bathing in the stream
Which is no road, because

Alas, there is no road to Grace's house!

I CHOSE MY TITLE, 'To Credit Marvels' from one of the seminal poems
in the work of Seamus Heaney. Not because, like Thomas Merton's
'Grace's House' it is inspired by a picture but because it suggests
something important in the work of great poetry. In Heaney's career
it marks the moment he begins to move from the death-centred
earth to the freedom of the air, from the unredeemed physicality
of nature to the secret places where deeper mysteries are at play.
The journey from books whose titles reveal the journey: *Death of a
Naturalist* to *The Spirit Level*. Remembering a painting of windmills and
canals and the heaviness of earth and water he writes:

My silting hope. My lowlands of the mind.
Heaviness of being. And poetry
Sluggish in the doldrums of what happens.
Me waiting until I was nearly fifty
To credit marvels. Like the tree-clock of tin cans

The tinkers made. So long for air to brighten,
Time to be dazzled and the heart to lighten.

Merton, too, is nearing fifty when 'Grace's House' is written and it is part of a collection of poetry, *Emblems of a Season of Fury* which include poems angry and apocalyptic "in the doldrums of what happens", but also poems which dance to fresh, bracing air. It is a vital collection for Merton. It opens the way for the final two poetic achievements of his life, *Cables to the Ace* and *The Geography of Lograire*. In those works he finds a way to bring together all elements of his poetry and life and produce two sustained masterpieces whose importance is only slowly being recognised. The long kaleidoscope structures allowed him to bring into creative tension the land and the air, the weight of guilt and the freedom of grace, history and hope. In *Emblems of a Season Of Fury* we find several poems continuing Merton's explorations of the possibilities of anti-poetry which started with 'Original Child Bomb' (1962). These would include 'A Picture of Lee Ying', 'Chant to be used in Processions around a Site with Furnaces'. Generally it is accepted that Nicanor Parra is the founder of the Anti-Poem, but in a 1965 letter to him Merton says:

> I am happy that you are thinking about maybe translating some poems of mine: you will find that before knowing your work I had written some antipoems.

Indeed the influence of the poetry of South America will play like pan music to much of *Emblems* and reach orchestral level in his *A Letter to Pablo Antonio Cuadro Concerning Giants*. There also you will find his *Hagia Sophia*. This central text in Merton's life is many ways another version of 'Grace's House'. The happy coincidence of Grace's name (Jung's 'synchronicity') echoes the feminine principle of God which is lingered on and explored in *Hagia Sophia*. The poems of wonder in *Emblems* include some of the abiding poems of Merton's career. As well as 'Grace's House' we have also 'Song for Nobody', 'Love Winter when the Plant says Nothing', 'The Fall' and, supremely, 'Night-Flowering Cactus'. They are all poems of Eden, poems that attempt to name the earth in fresh, childlike innocence. To cut through the metaphors and similes and say that we do exist in a redeemed world. If the anti-poetry is a powerful way of telling the hard truth about the "disgrace" of so many events in our history, those counterbalancing poems are efforts to speak the moments when redemption, grace, pours like rain on Kentucky woods. So many influences are at work in giving Merton the freedom to write this new poetry. Obviously the draw of South America, also the enigmatic simplicity of Chuang Tzu and Merton's deep sympathy with the poetry of Louis Zukovsky. His later article on Zukovsky will be called 'The Paradise Ear' and it is a self-descriptive title also for the Merton of those poems.

The background of 'Grace's House' is simple. A letter from her father, a Quaker, includes a drawing by his five year old daughter, Grace. The first four verses are a quiet description of the drawing. Smoke rolls from the chimney, the blades of grass and the flowers are counted, the dog is caught with his foreleg curled. But even in those verses there are clues to something deeper. The girl's name in the title. The first phrase "On the summit" suggests some overview of creation. "No blade of grass is not counted" echoes with the phrase of Jesus Christ: "Not a hair of your head is not counted". Twelve flowers has its own biblical undertones in the sacred number. The final devastating line of the whole poem is already given in three lines of verse two: "There is no path to the summit–/No path drawn/ To Grace's house". Here it is merely descriptive. Later, finally it becomes prescriptive, theological.

Verse Five introduces the world: "And there: the World!" It is a world seemingly benign—it sends Valentines for Grace. But Valentine cards are only a game, a pretence. Indeed part of the advertising world which will be one of the *tesserae* that make the mosaic of Merton's later work. At the end of Verse Five we find ourselves somewhere radically different. It is the first clue to the Eden theme of the poem. "There is a name on the ox, name of a family/ Not yet ready to be written in language". It is the time before the Fall, before the command to name the earth, to give titles to the animals etc. Paradise will not be specifically mentioned until Verse Eight: "O Paradise, O child's world!" but it is now established. That phrase from Verse Eight will echo around the last years of Merton's life. His hermitage will become his own 'Grace's House' and there he will enter fully the Blakean age of Innocence before the mystery of life. His article on Zukovsky will say:

> The speech of the child is paradise speech for it familiarly addresses all things, not yet knowing them as alien and anticipating nothing from them but joy...

'Grace's House' only very tentatively suggests the alien world beyond "this archetypal hill". The "spangled arrow" "Points from our Coney Island / To her green sun-hill" is a war-dance on other summits at the beginnings of the conquest of America, and Coney Island is the New York of *Lograire*. Indeed some of the geographical divisions of *Lograire* will emerge in Verse Eight. "The huge sun, bigger than the house / Stands and streams with life in the east / While in the west a thunder cloud / Moves away forever". At once just a comment on the child's drawing, but it implicates his own movement towards the East and his long, lifelong, involvement in the critique of the "thunder clouds" of war and nuclear weaponry.

Verse Nine names the child-vision as "This womb of mysteries" and again there is a hint of the Christ image of the need for rebirth if we are to know God, to be aware of grace everywhere. This vital awareness is directly stated in the preceding verse: "And all the animals are aware". One is reminded of the Buddhist notion of "mindfulness" which would have such a profound influence on Thomas Merton. The final two verses gather up the two elements of the poem. More items from the drawing are placed: "I must not omit to mention a rabbit / And two birds, bathing in the stream…" In every major poet (and I believe that from this collection on, Merton is that) every word chosen enters the magnetic field of attraction. They draw in other uses of those words and here we are feeling the pull of "the birds of appetite and paradise" and the birds which are his companions in the woods. The stream inevitably must be the Heraklitean river, that stream which is the very landscape of his entire life. His willingness to trust himself to a "river which is never crossed twice". 'Grace's House' develops this theme in its last lines: "And two birds, bathing in a stream / Which is no road, because / Alas, there is no road to Grace's house!".

This poem will have other effects. It will become the title poem of a German selection of his poetry (with an interesting introduction by Hans Urs von Balthasar). A choice which delighted Merton. It will also become the source of two letters (one to Grace's father, Elbert R. Sisson, and the other to Mark Van Doren) which will be among the 'Cold War Letters' (94 & 99). Some five years later in a letter to Grace herself, Merton will include a phrase which in turn will become the title of one of the Volumes of his Letters, "Road to Joy".

I would like to finish this reflection with that letter. It gives us the heart of the poem, it also reveals the heart of Merton, the reason we are here today, the reason he will continue to be one of the few who spoke the truth of our century out of his immersion in truths beyond this century, beyond time, out of the paradise eye and ear of one who recovered his childhood before the God who walked in Eden in the cool of the evening. The letter was written in May 1967.

> Of course I remember you and your drawing. If I did not answer in a big hurry, it was because I have a lot of letters to answer and have a difficult time doing that. But I want especially to thank you for your note and for your new drawing which is very significant. I like the way you see all the little creatures tending towards a tree which is a sort of tree of life. I am glad you still draw things with love and I hope you will never lose that. But I hope that you and I together will secretly travel our own road to joy, which is mysteriously revealed to us without our exactly realising. When I say that, I don't want you to start thinking about it. You already know it without thinking about it.

So do we all, thanks to Thomas Merton. Thank You.

Louisville Airport, May 5, 1966

CHRISTINE M. BOCHEN

Louisville Airport, May 5, 1966

Here on the foolish grass
Where the rich in small jets
Land with their own hopes
And their own kind

We with the gentle liturgy
Of shy children have permitted God
To make again His first world
Here on the foolish grass
After the spring rain has dried
And all the loneliness

Is for a moment lost in this simple
Liturgy of children permitting God
To make again that love
Which is His alone

His alone and terribly obscure and rare
Love walks gently as a deer
To where we sit on this green grass
In the marvel of this day's going down
Celebrated only
By all the poets since the world began.

This is God's own love He makes in us
As all the foolish rich fly down
Onto this paradise of grass
Where the world first began
Where God began
To make His love in man and woman

For the first time
Here on the sky's shore
Where the eternal sun goes down
And all the millionaires in small jets
Land with their own hopes
And their own kind

We with the tender liturgy
And tears
Of the newborn
Celebrate the first creation
Of solemn love
Now for the first time forever
Made by God in these
Four wet eyes and cool lips
And worshipping hands
When one voiceless beginning
Of splendid fire
Rises out of the heart
And the evening becomes One Flame
Which all the prophets
Accurately foresaw
Would make things plain
And create the whole world
Over again

There is only this one love
Which is now our world
Our foolish grass
Celebrated by all the poets
Since the first beginning
Of any song.

'Louisville Airport, May 5, 1966,' is the first of five poems published
in *Learning to Love*, Volume Six of Merton's journals. Also included in
the journal are 'I Always Obey My Nurse,' written on May 8, 1966;
'Aubade on a Cloudy Morning,' written on May 13, 1966; 'Certain
Proverbs Arise Out of Dreams,' written on May 18, 1966; and 'A
Long Call is Made Out of Wheels,' written on September 10, 1966.

These poems are among eighteen poems inspired by Merton's
love for M., the student nurse assigned to care for Merton during his
hospitalization for back surgery in late March 1966. Though he

recognized the private nature of the poems – for example, Merton notes that 'Louisville Airport, May 5, 1966' was "of course unpublishable" and "for M. only" – he could not resist sharing the poems with others as well. In April, he read one of the earlier poems 'With the World in My Bloodstream' to his novices, noting that "though I am sure that most of them did not understand much of it, they all seemed very attentive and moved—some (whom I would not have expected to be so) quite visibly." Merton added that the novices were "happy that I should share a poem with them—which I never do." In June, he shared some of the poems with his friends Victor and Carolyn Hammer and they talked about the possibility of printing the poems. They discussed the possibility of printing "a very elegantly edited, strictly limited edition: a real work of art. Not more than fifty or sixty copies in all." Of course, the author's identity would have to be "carefully concealed." Even though he wondered if that could be done, he hoped so. "Few people will have had such a memorial to their living love." In 1985, two hundred and fifty copies of *Eighteen Poems* were printed in a handsome edition arranged by Merton's friend Jay Laughlin. Merton had entrusted the poems and other personal papers to Laughlin for safekeeping.

Eighteen Poems has been the subject of two important essays: one by Douglas Burton-Christie published in *Crosscurrents* and a paper by Bonnie Thurston presented at the 1998 meeting of The Thomas Merton Society of Great Britain and Ireland, published in *Thomas Merton: Poet, Monk, Prophet*. Although, as Bonnie Thurston noted, the volume may not represent Merton's best poetry, *Eighteen Poems* certainly constitutes an important source for understanding Merton's own reading of this period in his life. Merton himself insists that the poems come closer than the journals to expressing what was in his heart. The love poems express something of the intensity of passion that Merton felt and witness to his efforts to celebrate and make sense of the love that was at once the source of deep joy and great anguish.

'Louisville Airport, May 5, 1966' was written a little more than a month after Merton met M. during a hospitalization for back surgery. They fell in love quickly. Although they had exchanged letters and talked on the phone, May 5 was only the second time they had been together following Merton's release from the hospital.

On May 5, Jay Laughlin, Nicanor Parra and Merton took M. to the Luau Room of the Louisville Airport. Merton described the scene this way: M. was

> more lovely than ever. I had on only my Trappist overalls but anyhow we got into the Luau Room at the airport. Lots of rich people were arriving for the Derby (which is today) and the place was full of brass and money and there I sat having a marvelous time, looking like a convict, unable to turn my head to see all the swanky jets landing beside me, satisfied to look at M.. I could hardly eat anything—not unusual as it has been that way since the operation.
>
> After supper M. and I had a little while alone and went off by ourselves and found a quiet corner, sat on the grass out of sight and loved each other to ecstasy. It was beautiful, awesomely so, to love so much and to be loved, and to be able to say it all completely without fear and without observation (not that we sexually consummated it).
>
> Came home dazed, long after dark (highly illegal!) and wrote a poem before going to bed. I think Nicanor Parra was highly edified. He was saying something about how one must "follow the ecstasy!"—by which he meant evidently right out of the monastery and over the hill. This of course I cannot do.

In an interview with Thomas McDonnell, published in March 1968, Merton remarked that "there are moments in human love in which loneliness is completely transcended but," he cautions, "these are brief and deceptive." Perhaps this evening at Louisville Airport on May 5, 1966 was one of those moments of transcendence—albeit a transitory one for both Merton and M.. Both wrote about their time together: Merton in a poem and M. in a letter to Merton from which he quotes in his journal:

> I want to be with you, to never be without you...I want to live with you darling! I want to share everything in your existence, I can't bear separation. To love you, to walk hand in hand, with you straight to God.

Merton comments, "She breaks my heart. How can we possibly be together unless I leave this place and how can I possibly get out of here? I really would if it were possible." Remember this phrase "if it were possible." M. imagines a future in which they walk "hand in hand to God" and Merton, who knows a future is impossible, celebrates the present moment in a poem. Both spiritualize their experience, drawing on the language of faith. Merton begins 'Louisville Airport, May 5, 1966' this way:

Here on the foolish grass
Where the rich in small jets
Land with their own hopes
And their own kind.

We with the gentle liturgy
Of shy children have permitted God
To make again that first world
Here on the foolish grass
After the spring rain has dried
And all the loneliness

Is for a moment lost in that simple
Liturgy of children permitting God
To make again that love which is His alone.

His alone and terribly obscure and rare
Love walks gently as a deer
To where we sit on the green grass
In the marvel of this day's going down
Celebrated only
By all the poets since the world began.

What for the millionaires landing in their swanky jets is just an airfield becomes for Merton and M. a patch of paradise: "the paradise of grass / where the world first began."

Merton describes the encounter as "a gentle liturgy" celebrating God's "first creation of solemn love." For this brief time the Garden of Eden is recreated and Merton and M. become the innocent first couple in the garden. Their love-making becomes "liturgy"—an act of worship and thanksgiving in which God works in them. For as Merton sees it, it is God who is making again "that love which is His alone." Their love is God's creation:

This is God's love He makes in us
As all the foolish rich fly down
Onto the paradise of grass
Where the world first began
Where God began
To make His love in man and woman
For the first time
Here on the sky's shore
Where the eternal sun goes down
And all the millionaires in small jets

Land with their own hopes
And their own kind.

Merton draws on his own experience, expressed in the poem, when in an essay called 'Love and Need' he writes: "Love is not a deal, it is a sacrifice. It is not marketing, it is a form of worship." Love is not only worship of the beloved but also worship of God. Human love is lifted up to God – the human and divine become one – through God's creative act—as it was when the world began. Merton and M. recover paradise—if only for a moment. They are born anew:

We with the tender liturgy
And tears
Of the newborn
Celebrate the first creation
Of solemn love
Now for the first time forever
Made by God in these
Four wet eyes and cool lips
And worshipping hands
When the one voiceless beginning
Of a splendid fire
Rises out of the heart
And all the evening is one flame
Which all the prophets
Accurately foresaw
Would make life plain
And create the whole world
Over again

Their simplicity and innocence stand in sharp contrast to the foolishness of the rich who "fly down / on to the paradise of grass" and see merely an airfield. Merton differs from them not only in dress (recall the overalls) but in vision. He sees something the others do not see.

The symbolism of liturgy/creation/paradise allows Merton to celebrate his love for M. as a gift from God and, for just a few moments, to stay with the ecstasy. In this poem, as in the seventeen others, Merton expresses his love for M. in the language of faith, finding in myth and symbol the words with which to share what is in his heart and to say what is on his mind. The imagery of new creation and new birth serves him well.

There is only the one love
Which is now our world

Our foolish grass
Celebrated by all
The poets since the first beginning
Of any song.

But it is not a relationship that can last. A few months later, in another of the *Eighteen Poems* included in the journal, he would express both resolution and longing as in 'For M. in October,' as he wrote:

"If only you and I
Were possible."

Cargo Catechism

Paul M. Pearson

Cargo Catechism

1. Here is how it all began. Old Anut made him some man and woman along flowers animals trees fish putem in a garden belong plenty canned beef ricebags (polished) instant coffee, tobacco matches and candybars. Old man and woman no pants and lots of whiskey. Baimbai plenty pekato mekim plenty trabel. Nogut. Old Anut took away all the canned food before they could even find the canopener. Quick lockup garden and hide all the whiskey. You wantem inferno Ol Man Adam? "Suppose you spik: I no got inferno, baimbai you go along IN."

2. Noah was a gutfela so Old Anut showed him how to build a steamer. Make him strongfela talk: get along steamer with plenty Cargo along all animals quick I make him rain longtime no can finish. Noah had a peaked cap white shirt shorts stockings and shoes. The rain came down and Noah rang the bell and off went the steamer with all the animals that's all. Steamer belong plenty canned beef ricebags (polished) instant coffee tobacco matches and candybars. No whiskey. Old Noah always properly dressed. Nix pekato. Nix trabel.

3. Baimbai rain stops and steamer lands in Australia. Old Noah finds a bottle of whiskey lying around Sydney. Bad news for everybody that's all. Noah want 'em one drink work him trouble no can finish. One drink takes off shoes. Two drinks takes off the socks. Son Ham belongs Noah watches and laughs when old boy takes off his pants.

For this Ham is deprived of cargo, canned meat, razor-blades etc and sent to New Guinea to be a black man. Shem and Japheth remain white, keep the Cargo and remain in Sydney.

Cargo Catechism is taken from the East canto of The Geography of Lograire. This poem, along with Cables to the Ace and others of Merton's antipoems is frequently regarded as some of the most complicated and inaccessible poetry Merton wrote. Yet, to regard these poems as a temporary aberration as George Woodcock did in his critical study of Merton is to ignore a central strand of Merton's literary output, and one that occupied him for the final years of his life as a hermit.

I have chosen to explore a short section of *Lograire* entitled 'Cargo Catechism.' Initially I found it one of the most incomprehensible parts of the poem. This changed for me in two ways. Firstly when I tried reading some sections of it aloud and the text itself came to life and secondly, upon reading some of the sources Merton was using in writing this poem and beginning to come to an understanding of what Merton was attempting to do in this canto and in the poem as a whole.

Cargo Catechism is composed of nine prose paragraphs all written in a similar style using pidgin English. The first paragraph is based on a New Guinea story concerning the creation of the world which begins in a similar style to Genesis: "Here is how it all began..." and the fall is attributed to sex and whiskey—the latter not normally referred to in the traditional Genesis story! The following paragraphs tell the story of Noah and the flood, and then Ham's sin of seeing his father naked which leads to the division of the races with Ham being sent to New Guinea as a black man and his brothers, Shem and Japheth remaining in Sydney. The remaining paragraphs explore the attempts to obtain cargo for themselves by the descendants of Ham.

In these paragraphs Merton has combined stories and words from anthropological literature[1] about the cults, with some of his own stories and words he has created in his own version of pidgin English.

In other sections of the East Canto of *Lograire* Merton explores a number of different manifestations of the cargo cults and explores the ways the natives coped with cultural change and fought – literally at times – to improve their lot and to gain access to the whiteman's cargo.

So, a little background information about cargo cults and then I'll go on to suggest briefly what I think Merton is attempting to achieve by incorporating them into *Lograire*.

Cargo Cults are Messianic, mystical, eschatological movements. They originated in New Guinea and Melanesia around the end of the nineteenth century and were still in existence up until the early nineteen-fifties, with sporadic appearances as late as 1965.[2]

Strictly speaking cargo cults are means by which primitives and underprivileged people believe they can obtain manufactured goods by an appeal to supernatural powers—ancestors, spirits, etc. Through the coming of the missionaries and political administrators in the nineteenth century up until the return of the whiteman after the defeat of Japan in the second world war, natives had seen how cargo had arrived for the whiteman by sea and, ultimately, with the coming of the Americans after the war, by air.

The natives desire for cargo is not solely because they desire material things. They desire it because it will establish them as equal to the white man and give them an identity as respectable as his. They also desire it because they have become increasingly dependent on western goods so that, as old skills have been lost, western goods have changed from a luxury to a necessity—a process continually taking place in western culture. Cargo shows, or is seen as a proof of, their own fundamental worth.

The cults teach that the white man has a special means of communication with God, and that, if the native learns this special secret, he too will be able to share in these blessings. They do not have cargo as a result of some wrong-doing on their part—in this section it is attributed to Ham's sin of seeing his father, Noah, naked. So the story of Noah is incorporated by the natives into their own myth-dream as a means of explaining the apparent superiority of the whiteman and their own lack of cargo. Cargoism is a means for the native to assert their sense of personal worth—these stories contain a demand for dignity. *Lograire* presents a panorama of human exploitation – western, first world culture, encountering other cultures and destroying their myth-dreams – Mayan Indians, Native Americans or, in this case, Cargo Cults.

The natives had observed the way white men sign and stamp papers. As a result of this ritual, boats or planes arrived carrying the goods which affirmed them as the superior race, including their laws, their administration, their religion and the guns they used to enforce their position. Another occurrence was based on the natives observations of how the white men decorated their homes with vases of flowers, and they copied this in the hope of receiving Cargo.[3] Cargo gave the white man status in the eyes of the natives. But such myths continue in our own culture today—people become rich through dealing in stocks and shares and gambling on the stock market or marking the right numbers on a lottery ticket. Electronic commerce enables those who understand the technology, who speak the "hyper text mark-up language" to be the new entrepreneurs.

Besides illustrating an historical aspect of human exploitation Merton also uses the Cargo Cults as yet one more way of parodying the exploitative nature of western culture, especially modern advertising. For the natives, the desire for access to the whiteman's sources for Cargo symbolised what they felt was essential to the greater fulfillment of their life, yet was missing. So Merton can ask: "Is there really much difference, though, between kago and the coming of the good life promised in our fabulous modern consumer advertising?" (Love and Living, 83) Advertising projects images of a better life, of endless possessions and portrays a Western myth-dream of what is needed for happiness. Goods that were once satisfactory are "suddenly discovered to be inadequate, obsolete" even though they still function. A need to be on the information superhighway, to be information rich not poor. Yet there is a striking image from Bill Clinton's recent visit to India of Indian villagers stressing their need to be connected to the internet, whilst still not having a proper connection to a fresh water supply.

Merton concluded his essay on 'Cargo Cults of the South Pacific' by suggesting that the native and the white man need each other "to co-operate in the common enterprise of building a world adequate for the historical maturity of man." For this to be possible we first have to be in touch with our inner self and understand the myth-dreams that operate in our own life and culture.[4] When we are aware of these myth-dreams we will be able to recognise the myth-dreams of others. We will be able to avoid our myth-dreams turning into the nightmares of violence, war and racism, instead overcoming disunity and creating real relationships and true community with respect and tolerance for the stranger.

Notes and References

The literature Merton was studying is still essential reading for anthropology students today.

1. The Prophet Malik Movement on New Hanover Island occurred in 1964-5. Malik prophesied that Lyndon Johnson would arrive aboard the Queen Mary,

laden with cargo for the islanders. When this did not happen some Australian police posts on the island were attacked to punish them for "stealing the cargo."

2. When the natives began to copy this practice the whiteman became nervous and forbade it.

3. The belief that dignity has something to do with possessions, cargo, is ultimately a white myth.

Bibliography

Burridge, Kenelm. *Mambu: A Melanesian Millenium*. London: Methuen, 1960.

Lawrence, Peter. *Road Belong Cargo: A Study of the Cargo Movement in the Southern Madang District New Guinea*. Manchester: Manchester University Press, 1964.

Merton, Thomas. *The Geography of Lograire*. New York: New Directions, 1969.

Merton, Thomas. *Love and Living*. Edited by Naomi Burton Stone and Patrick Hart. London, Sheldon Press, 1979.

Murphy, John J. *The Book of Pidgin English*. Rev. ed. Brisbane: Smith and Paterson, 1966.

Padovano, Anthony T. *The Human Journey: Thomas Merton, Symbol of a Century*. Garden City, N.Y.: Image Books, 1982.

Worsley, Peter. *The Trumpet Shall Sound: A Study of Cargo Cults in Melanesia*. 2nd Edition. London: Paladin, 1970.

THOMAS MERTON
a mind awake in the dark

PAPERS & WORKSHOPS

Marriage of East and West:
The Contribution of
Thomas Merton and Bede Griffiths
to Inter-religious Dialogue

PATRICK W. H. EASTMAN

THIS PAPER IS NOT GOING TO BE A COMPARISON BETWEEN THOMAS Merton and Bede Griffiths but rather an indication of the invaluable contribution that both have made to the impetus of today's exchanges between Christians, Buddhists and Hindus. Although this paper will give exclusive attention to these two monastics, this by no means implies that they were the only pioneers in this field.

Alan Griffiths (to use his baptismal name) was born at Walton-on-Thames in 1906. He attended Oxford University and after his first year switched his studies from Philosophy to English Literature. C.S. Lewis was his tutor and the two of them became good friends. In his early days at University Bede rejected religion, but towards the end of his time at Oxford he became aware of a sense of the 'holy' and the 'inner source of life'. It is worth noting that both Bede and Merton had a mystical experience completely out of the blue when, as teenagers, they had no real religious affiliation or inclination. Bede recounts how the world came alive for him as he walked alone one evening in the playing fields at his school(GS, p.9). Merton vividly describes his experience of the mosaics and churches in Rome that drives him to his knees(SSM, p.116ff.).

After university Alan and two friends began an experiment in simple, community life in a small cottage in rural England. Through reading the Bible, Alan rediscovered the Christian faith and became active in the Church of England, even considering ordination to the priesthood. After a whole night on his knees in prayer in 1933 he decided to join the Roman Catholic Church and within a month entered the Benedictine Monastery at Prinknash, taking 'Bede' as his religious name. After many years in monastic life he became guestmaster at Pluscarden Abbey where he met Toni Sussman, and under her influence Bede began reading the sacred texts of the East. These studies created a longing to go to India.

In 1955 Bede was given permission to respond to an invitation from Fr Benedict Alapatt, an Indian Benedictine, to establish a Benedictine foundation in the Bangalore region of South India. As he was preparing to leave Britain, Bede summed up his desire in a letter to a friend: "I'm going out to India to seek the other half of my soul." This statement expresses the pressing lack he felt both in himself and in his culture. Britain, like most of the Western world steeped in Graeco-Roman and Cartesian philosophy and psychology, was far too addicted to the rational, analytic mind. It gave little room to spirituality and the interiority of contemplation. Even in his monastery, where these values were espoused, there was no method for accessing them directly. At first things did not go well in India, but in 1958 Bede joined with a Belgian Cistercian named Fr Frances Mahieu in establishing Kurisumala Ashram in Kerala.

After ten years at Kurisumala, Bede responded, in 1968, to an invitation from Fr Henri le Saux (Abhishiktananda) to take charge of Saccidananda Ashram at Shantivanam (Forest of Peace) founded by le Saux and another French priest, Jules Monchanin in 1950. It was at this Ashram, dedicated to the Holy Trinity, that Father Bede established a deeply Christian contemplative lifestyle thoroughly inculturated in a simple Indian way. It was here that he extensively studied Sanskrit, the Hindu sacred writings and traditions, while also engaging in inter-religious dialogue. Under Bede's leadership a solid community grew that eventually affiliated with the Congregation of Camaldolese Benedictines. This community, with its regular round of monastic prayer, formed the heart of the Ashram which began to attract spiritual seekers from all over the world.

Father Bede died on May 13, 1993. On hearing of his death Cardinal Basil Hume of Westminster said of him:

> We can only stand in admiration of the way in which Dom Bede Griffiths, throughout his life and holding us all in prayer, explored the origins of all religions. He is a source of inspiration and encouragement

for many all over the world, since he is a mystic in touch with absolute love and beauty.

We turn now to Thomas Merton. According to William Healy, Merton's interest in Eastern religions began with a college reading of Huxley's *Ends and Means*. We can also note from Merton's autobiography *The Seven Storey Mountain* that while at Columbia University he knew of Father Wieger's French translation of oriental texts. During the late 1930s Merton had contact with a Hindu monk, Bramachari, who not only introduced him to Eastern Spirituality but also to the classic texts of Western Spirituality. You may remember from his autobiography that when he entered the Roman Catholic Church Merton had some pretty negative things to say about Eastern religions.

> Ultimately, I suppose all Oriental mysticism can be reduced to techniques that do the same thing, but in a far more subtle and advanced fashion: and if that is true, it is not mysticism at all. It remains purely in the natural order. That does not make it evil, per se, according to Christian standards: but it does not make it good, in relation to the supernatural. It is simply more or less useless, except when it is mixed up with elements that are strictly diabolical. (SSM, p.205-6)

It would seem that in 1949 his interest in the East was rekindled when he met a man who had come to do some painting at Gethsemani who had been a postulant in a Zen monastery in Hawaii and had spoken to the community about it in chapter.

By the late 1950s Merton was seriously studying the writings of the Japanese Zen master, D.T. Suzuki. Merton now clearly had a vastly different assessment of the Eastern tradition and from now on there are frequent references to Zen in his journal. Perhaps he now felt that he was well rooted enough in his Christian tradition to be comfortable at entering into dialogue with Suzuki and others. To be rooted in one's own tradition is vital for satisfactory dialogue. It is important to remember that both Bede and Merton always thought of themselves as thoroughly Christian. As Brother David Steindl-Rast has pointed out: *Merton could go so deeply into another tradition only because he had a home to which he could return.* Both Bede and Merton always remained rooted in their Christian tradition and teach us a valuable lesson for any activity in which we might engage towards inter-religious dialogue.

Merton records receiving a letter from Suzuki in his Journal on April 11, 1959. After noting the contents of the letter in a very positive way, Merton continues with words that are absolutely central to all inter-religious dialogue.

> If I tried baldly and bluntly to 'convert' Suzuki, that is, make him 'accept' formulas regarding the faith that are accepted by the average American Catholic, I would, in fact, not 'convert' him at all, but simply confuse and (in a cultural sense) degrade him.

> On the contrary – if I can meet him on a common ground of spiritual Truth, where we share a real and deep experience of God, and where we know in humility our own deepest selves – and if we can discuss and compare the formulas we use to describe this experience, then I certainly think Christ would be present and glorified in both of us, and this would lead to a *conversion of us both*. (Vol.3, Journal p.273)

Merton had a chance to put this into action when he met Suzuki in New York in 1964. He accepted Suzuki just as he was and a genuine dialogical exchange was able to take place. This openness and the feeling of being "at home" with Suzuki which he describes in his journal entry of that meeting is no doubt because Zen gave Merton a language to articulate his own contemplative experience. Through his contact with Suzuki, Merton wrote a seminal work in Buddhist-Christian studies entitled *Zen and the Birds of Appetite* and a collection of essays *Mystics and Zen Masters*.

We should not think that Merton's interest in Eastern religion lacked the praxis of Bede who had immersed himself in the culture and spirituality of India. Merton incorporated Zen practice into his meditation. Through this he was able, like Bede, to recover the ancient tradition of contemplation and interiority in Christianity. Zen provided Merton with a whole range of techniques and exercises for facilitating the spiritual journey. It can be noted that Merton's attraction to the East was for similar reasons as Bede. Bonnie Thurston remarks in her essay 'Why Merton Looked East' that:

> Merton was increasingly disgusted with technological, materialistic America and the Eastern Way provided an alternative to its 'getting and keeping' mentality. Merton came to believe that the modern West lacked interiority. Buddhism, with its ancient practices and profound formulations of religious psychology, gave Merton a new and enriching collection of prayer practices. Merton adopted and adapted Buddhist prayer techniques into Christian practice. (TCW)

We will never know for certain how much Bede and Merton influenced the Second Vatican Council's revolutionary document,

The Declaration on the Relation of the Church to Non-Christian Religions (Nostra Aetate).

There we read:

> Thus, in Hinduism people explore the divine mystery and express it both in the limitless riches of myth and the accurately defined insights of philosophy. They seek release from the trials of the present life by ascetical practices, profound meditation and recourse to God in confidence and love...

> The Catholic Church rejects nothing of what is true and holy in these religions. She has a high regard for the manner of life and conduct, the precepts and doctrines which, although differing in many ways from her own teaching, nevertheless often reflect a ray of that truth which enlightens all...

> The Church, therefore, urges her children to enter with prudence and charity into discussion and collaboration with members of other religions. Let Christians, while witnessing to their own faith and way of life, acknowledge, preserve and encourage the spiritual and moral truths found among non-Christians, also their social life and culture.

Merton gives us further orientation to the task of inter-religious dialogue in his *Asian Journal*. There are two extremely significant passages

> ...I think we have now reached a stage of (long-overdue) religious maturity at which it may be possible for someone to remain perfectly faithful to a Christian and Western monastic commitment, and yet to learn in depth from, say, a Buddhist or Hindu discipline and experience. (AJ, p.313)

Merton also writes:

> And I believe that by openness to Buddhism, to Hinduism, and to these great Asian traditions, we stand a wonderful chance of learning more about the potentiality of our own traditions, because they have gone, from the natural point of view, so much deeper into this than we have. (AJ, p.343)

Merton died in 1968 and Bede in 1993. We would do well to ask whether their contribution and influence still continues. In this paper I will list a few of the ways in which their work for inter-religious dialogue is still alive. Both our subjects published a number of books on the religious traditions of the East. Both Merton and Bede have given us many foundational writings upon which contemporary scholars continue to build. Academic theses on the subject continue to be produced and conferences, workshops and retreats abound using the life and writings of both of these two Christian monastic figures that were held in such high esteem by the religious leaders of the non-Christian East.

Building on their work, and especially on Merton is the Aide-Inter-Monastères and its sub-division Dialog-Inter-Monastères both based in Paris guided by Dom Pierre de Béthune OSB. The Monastic Interreligious Dialogue composed of Benedictines and Cistercians in North America has made a very significant contribution. This latter organization has done much to further dialogue especially with their monastic exchange program between Buddhists and Christians. This culminated in 1996 with a ground breaking gathering of Christian and Buddhist monks with His Holiness the Dalai Lama and other Buddhist leaders for an Encounter at Gethsemani. Dom Pierre in his preface to the book of published papers from the meeting states rightly that "The Buddhist-Christian encounter at Gethsemani will remain as a reference point for the future of interfaith dialogue." In his Foreword to the same book the Dalai Lama, who incidentally asked that it be held at Merton's own monastery, writes:

> Gatherings of spiritual practitioners from different backgrounds, such as the Gethsemani Encounter, are of immense value. I believe it is extremely important that we extend our understanding of each other's spiritual practices and traditions. This is not necessarily done in order to adopt them ourselves, but to increase our opportunities for mutual respect. Sometimes, too, we encounter something in another tradition that helps us better appreciate something in our own. Consequently, I hope that Christians, Buddhists, people of all faiths and people without faith will approach this book from the Gethsemani Encounter with the same rigorous curiosity and courage for which Thomas Merton was renowned. (GE, p.ix)

My recent visit to Dom Bede's Ashram in India convincingly showed that it continues to flourish. Bede's pattern of inculturation, contemplative life and inter-religious dialogue continues to attract numerous guests from all over the world. The work of social outreach to the local community is impressive. The Camaldolese Benedictine community there carry on the tradition of Bede. We need such places because rather than on the level of theological debate the truth and enrichment of inter-religious dialogue is only obtained by entering into the contemplative dimension. As Father Bede said,

What we find is that if you're arguing doctrines and so on, you get nowhere, but when you meet in meditation you begin to share your own inner experience and you begin to realize an underlying unity behind the religions. (from an unpublished lecture)

Bede would illustrate this in his talks by holding up his hand and beginning with his thumb point to each finger saying "Christianity, Judaism, Islam, Hinduism, Buddhism." At the finger tips he would show that Buddhism was far away from Christianity, yet, he would say pointing to his palm that as one goes to the depths in silent meditation one discovers their essential unity.

Osage Monastery near Tulsa in Oklahoma is a center that continues to bring Bede's insights, teachings and practice authentically to the West. Fr Bede himself encouraged and was very supportive of this Benedictine Ashram, founded in 1980 and ably directed by Benedictine Sister Pascaline Coff. A disciple of Bede, she is deeply formed in the monastic contemplative tradition and the Spirit of Father Bede.

I am personally convinced that over the next several generations all the world religions will be enriched and changed by three factors that are now just emerging. First is the increase of people desiring and recovering the mystical dimension of religion (pace Karl Rahner's assertion that the Christian of the future will either be a mystic or nothing). Secondly the advent of women of all religious traditions writing theology and being taken seriously, and finally inter-religious dialogue. Both Merton and Bede were supportive in all three of these and have already made a significant impact.

Our way forward is given direction by the words of Merton and Bede:

> The deepest level of communication is not communication, but communion. It is wordless. It is beyond words, and it is beyond speech, and it is beyond concept. Not that we discover a new unity. We discover an older unity…we are already one. But we imagine that we are not. And what we have to recover is our original unity. What we have to be is what we are. (AJ, p.308)

writes Merton in his *Asian Journal*, while Bede writes in *The Marriage of East and West*:

> When the mind in meditation goes beyond images and concepts, beyond reason and will to the ultimate Ground of its consciousness, it experiences itself in this timeless and spaceless unity of Being. The

Ultimate is experienced in the depth of the soul, in the substance or Center of its consciousness, as its own Ground or Source, as its very being or Self (Atman). This is an experience of self-Transcendence, which gives an intuitive insight into Reality. (MEW, p.31)

No doubt it was an awareness of this essential contemplative dimension that prompted Pope Paul VI to invite Benedictine and Cistercian monastics to be at the forefront of the dialogue with non-Christian religions. Hence we can say that all who have a contemplative lifestyle are included in this invitation.

Notes and References

AJ: Merton, Thomas. *The Asian Journal*. Sheldon Press, London, 1973.

GS: Griffiths, Bede. *The Golden String*. Templegate Publishers, Springfield, 1980.

GE: Mitchell, Donald W. & James Wiseman OSB, Editors. *The Gethsemani Encounter*. Continuum, New York, 1998.

Journal: Merton, Thomas. *The Search for Solitude – The Journals of Thomas Merton* Volume 3 (1952–1960). HarperSan Francisco, 1996.

MEW: Griffiths, Bede. *The Marriage of East and West*. Templegate Publishers, Springfield, 1982.

SSM: Merton, Thomas. *The Seven Storey Mountain*. Harcourt, Brace and Company, Inc., New York, 1948.

TCW: Thurston, Bonnie. *The Christian World*. May/June, 1989.

When the Light of the East Meets the Wisdom of the West

DANNY SULLIVAN

KIM WOLFE-MURRAY

[Editorial note: We have tried to capture the spirit of this recorded dialogue which Kim and Danny led without any notes.]

DS: WHEN KIM AND I WERE TALKING ABOUT DOING THIS SESSION, WE DECIDED NOT to do a paper because we know there's a sense in which people enjoy papers but also that people have said that they would like more dialogue and more engagement. We thought we'd be quite nonconformist and take a big risk and try and do that. We've made proper use of technology so we've been able to e-mail each other about our thoughts and about our ideas. What we are going to do is to begin a dialogue between us that eventually we would like people to feel free to join in with.

We chose the title because we have a sense that the Light of the East, the eastern tradition, eastern spirituality, has actually uncovered, quite remarkably, some of the jewels in the western spiritual tradition and in the Wisdom of the West. But we also believe that the wisdom of the western tradition of spirituality and particularly contemplative spirituality, whether it is monastic or lay, has reflected very positively and very imaginatively on the Light of the East...that it really has been a two-way process. And that has been very fruitful, we feel, between the two traditions.

I want to begin the dialogue with Kim by reminding him that in my early twenties, in terms of my spiritual life, I felt totally disorientated. Having come through a very fundamentalist, authoritarian Catholic upbringing and begun to let it go, I was

completely disorientated, as you might imagine. If you come from
that sort of background and upbringing and begin to let go of it, it
really is very frightening. It was a very difficult time for me. However
I began to find a sense of spiritual 'richedness' when I discovered
Samye Ling, the Tibetan monastery on the Scottish borders near
Eskdalemuir, a remarkable spiritual community with a real heart and
a real soul.

I discovered Samye Ling from a reference in Merton's *Asian Journal*
to the founder of the community. Merton, being Merton, had said "I
think that when I come back from India I might go via Scotland and
Wales and I'll see if I can visit that monastery in Scotland." So
I sought it out because it just struck a chord. And that began to
give me a sense of spiritual rootedness again and I seriously
contemplated becoming a Buddhist. Yet I think what stopped me
from becoming a Buddhist was Merton. It was that reference which
Patrick Eastman mentioned…that if you are going to engage with
another tradition or you are going to understand another tradition,
actually you must get much more firmly rooted in your own
tradition and understand it better. Something which His Holiness,
the Dalai Lama, always says to anybody who wants to be a Buddhist,
"Go and rediscover the jewels in your own tradition. Even if you are
irritated by it or angry with it, see if you can find something deeper."

So I did that. But what I didn't lose was my deep love and affection
for the Buddhist tradition and Buddhist practice. When I went to the
conference at Winchester, and this is a metaphor for seeing, Kim was
the only person I saw who was wearing monastic robes, as far as I
can remember. That was very interesting. The first thing I thought I
saw were the robes. And then I sat with him during a meal…and I
began to see the monk. And then following that, I began to see who
was behind the monk, who the person was. And that taught me
something about the metaphor of seeing. Now Merton in a sense
helped me not to become a Buddhist but [addressing Kim] I think
Merton in a sense influenced you into Buddhist monasticism…

KW-M: That was something I think I spoke about at the first Merton
conference. In early days when I first started to get into spirituality,
Merton was a very important influence. The breakthrough for me
really was through Buddhist meditation. That was the first time I

really got beneath the surface of religion. I happened to be working for a publisher who was in Edinburgh – my mother's publishing company – which had published a book called *Thomas Merton, Monk and Poet* which I think is quite hard to get hold of these days. I think I just recognised someone who came from a similar background, a slightly bohemian background, who had taken that journey into faith. So, as I was approaching Buddhist monasticism, I felt as though I had a companion there, someone who had gone down that road. There were so many parallels...the sense of Merton going from an extreme, hedonistic life, coming from a bohemian background, and then going into a very austere tradition. And of course, the tradition that I first came across, and it was pure chance, did happen to be one of the most austere forms of Buddhist monasticism around.

And I don't know what it is about me...but I think we were talking about this earlier...the idea of having to have a very powerful container for wild energy. There's a need for that. But what is behind that wild energy is actually spirituality...spiritual power...so I think that was a really strong connection that Danny and I made with each other when we first met. For both of us, in our own way, Merton had been a really important influence in our engagement with what became our spiritual home. And yet also, and I think that is what I really cherished about Merton, especially during the early days, but throughout my monastic life and also through the time since I've left, is that he gives you the ground from which to approach and go beyond your own tradition and almost challenges you to do that. That is something that we immediately saw in each other...we both had this connecting point across traditions partly through Merton's influence...

DS: Taking that further, one of the things that struck us in our dialogue before today was that Merton was very consistent and very gifted in 'seeing through'...seeing through the superficiality sometimes of structures, whether religious structures or secular structures, seeing through the superficiality of life as some people would regard it. And of course that again is a very rich aspect of the Buddhist tradition, not to be taken in by illusion, by what seems to be real, by what seems to be attractive. Also, in terms of practice, whether Buddhist or Christian, not to be taken in by thinking that now that you're on a path of practice, that it's about being a good practitioner or the best practitioner. That's very important.

I believe that we both think that, in terms of our contemporary world now, there is an awful lot to see through and in fact that there are a lot of, particularly, young people out there who are passionately interested in and wishing to be engaged in a sense of 'the spiritual', of what it is to be spiritual. But in one sense, organised religion, organised, institutionalised religion is not speaking to that. And, in fact they see through it and that's a challenge...

KW-M: I think that a lot of the dialogue that we were having in connection with this was in relation to Merton's relationship with the establishment. Merton was a man who practised silence...but he wasn't quiet. He was not passive in terms of his relationship to what he saw as wrongs within the establishment, within the organisation. That was a very important influence for me because I was working within a very highly structured and orthodox form of Buddhism which had a very strong spiritual part to it but, at the same time, one of the things that enabled me to engage with it was the whole teaching on Convention.

The idea in Buddhism that there is both 'conditioned reality' and 'unconditioned reality' means that one can use forms quite skilfully. Merton is a very good example of that, someone who perfected his form and was a very good monk. He was a disciplined monk. He mastered the form and that is not a simple thing to do. It is not an easy thing to do. And he didn't make anything out of it. From that mastery sprung his freedom. But then from that perspective, the perspective of experiencing freedom within the confines of a form, as Danny was saying, you start to see through the corruption within a form very quickly and very easily. So how do you relate to that? This is something I am very conscious of as someone grateful for what I have received from Merton: how do I practise that now within my life in the situation and the organisation that I'm involved with now?

Going back to the Buddhist influence within Christianity, something really strikes me when I come to conferences. On the one hand there's a great delight in hearing refined and disciplined minds talking about theological traditions within Christianity. At the same time it I find it very alien to me as a Buddhist because Buddhism is not based on belief. It doesn't depend upon a theological base to be developed before practice can be authentic. I think there was a reference earlier to one of Merton's comments when he first went into the monastery and talked in a disparaging way about the 'systems' within the oriental tradition saying that that was all that they amounted to. This is a very interesting area to explore because it can seem like that from the outside. In order to get your head around it, you have to understand the contemplative approach, the attitude needed in order to pick up those systems.

As far as the contemporary situation is concerned, how do we apply the teachings of Merton within our situation right now? Of course we need to understand the background and the history and the route that Merton followed but at the same time what does it actually all mean in practice now in our relationships with organisations, with society and with the social issues that are around us? I think that is, I suppose, the gauntlet that I would like to throw down to all of you. That's what makes this kind of conference so exciting. We feel that people are prepared to challenge existing structures in the way that Merton did.

DS: One of the areas we explored in relation to what Kim has just said is that what Buddhism has taught the western spiritual tradition is the importance of practice, daily practice, and how you take that daily practice into all the situations and people that you meet on a day-to-day basis. I was saying to Kim that when I was going through the interviews for the post that I'm taking up in September, I knew there was one person there who might make me feel uncomfortable, might even try and be intimidating. I said that it was my experience of Buddhist practice that allowed me to go into that situation and not be afraid. If I didn't get the job, I didn't get the job, but I was not going to be intimidated by that person. They were not going to make me feel afraid. And they did try to make me feel uncomfortable, they did try to do what I thought they might try to do.

We went on to say that if you take the practice seriously into your daily life, ultimately that's really what it's all about. The contemplative life can not be passive. Maybe what you're developing, and maybe we see this not only in the writings of Merton but of great writers within the Buddhist tradition, is that you begin to discover the arts of the spiritual revolutionary. Maybe that's what our world needs…the art of the spiritual revolutionary who will hold secular values, or stereotypical values or the way asylum seekers or homeless people are treated, will hold those values to hostage and say there's something not quite right about these, that we have got to negotiate and get back to a rootedness and something much more centred on a sense of the other and compassion for the other… Perhaps this is the point to open discussion up for people to engage in with their own ideas and thoughts.

Patrick Woodhouse: Arising out of your last remarks, Danny, I'm really glad you said that. It's terribly easy to become too spiritual in all this business. Thomas Merton in his own kind of anarchistic way upends our spirituality, doesn't he, and brings us back to earth and makes us face the issues of our day. One of the things that I found disturbing when I was in India, if I can introduce a note of contention, didn't involve the Buddhist tradition. I spent some time in north India in an ashram and it was when meeting Hindu swamis, particularly one whom *Time* magazine had voted one of the ten holiest men in the world. He lived in a monastery beside the river Jumna beyond Beredu. He hadn't spoken for fourteen years, had taken a vow of silence. I've read some of his literature and we managed to get to him and sit in his presence. We were ushered in and allowed to ask just one question. A French woman sat beside him and she was his amansuensis. He could speak but he never did. And so this was a way of actually not engaging in dialogue because if you can't speak, you just do it through your amansuensis.

But anyway the thing that we tussled over with him was this great doctrine of the realisation of the Self which as I understand from my very simple knowledge, is a cardinal idea in Hindu spirituality; to realise the Self. This sounds very near to what Merton talked about… finding the True Self. And yet one of the things that struck me as I listened to him was the almost, it seemed to me, total lack of engagement with history. The whole Judaeo-Christian tradition of engaging with the historical forces that shape and distort our world, the whole prophetic tradition, there just didn't seem to anything of that at all. In your worst moments, you begin to think that contemplation is a huge escape from engagement. Now for Merton that was never, ever, ever the case. I don't know enough about Bede Griffiths to know whether he had the same kind of prophetic thrust all the time... I'm not sure that he did. But the question I have, arising out of your last remarks, is how in one's practice one can keep alive the discernment that you're not becoming deluded in some kind of spiritual cul-de-sac but that you are constantly engaged with where people are hurting and suffering. Because it seems it can go either way...

DS: I think that you're absolutely right and I remember at the Good Heart, the three days with the Dalai Lama held by the Christian Meditation Movement, some very affluent young man in his mid-twenties who was used to quick fixes, being able to make quick decisions, almost asking the Dalai Lama for a quick fix, "I think all this is really a little bit...can you tell me how to do this, you know, like now!" The Dalai Lama first of all said, "Daily practice," and then said, "If on your spiritual path, it's good, it's joyful, it's wonderful, you're entirely happy...you are off it!" Because if you're really on the spiritual path, it's going to be about broken-ness, it's going to be about pain, it's going to be about suffering and it's going to be about always being willing to confront with that and to engage with it. I think you are absolutely right. Any contemplative tradition or spirituality which takes you away from that in some kind of superior sense of looking after other people but actually not engaging with their pain and their suffering is quite false. I still think that danger is really there and I think that you are absolutely right. It's not just there, in my view, within the Christian tradition. It can be in any tradition. Some way of coping is to just opt out but you actually think you're opting out in a very precious kind of a way.

Patrick Eastman: I was just going to respond about Bede Griffiths. I think that Bede saw the two-directional way in which things went. He worked a lot on the Advaitic tradition and its relationship to the Christian doctrine of the Trinity. In his writings and his reflections on that, of that sort of unitive experience and the oneness, he thought that it was not simply a vertical oneness as one God but that it brought about a oneness that, if it was authentic, had to be effected in or with relationship. Although I don't think he wrote as significantly and as prophetically on social issues as Merton did, his writings certainly continue to do prophetic work of spiritual revolution not so much through the community and the ashram but in undermining and cutting against, in a prophetic way, much of the system of caste and all of those things that separate and divide and are alienating. In a different way, Bede certainly would be at one with Merton in the realisation that to realise one's self can only be a realisation of oneself in the Other. One of Bede's favourite passages from St John's Gospel is that the Father and I are one. He sees that as that 'all is one', yet there is diversity in that oneness and the work is to establish the oneness.

KW-M: Can I just make a short response to Patrick's statement... which is a very familiar one from westerners approaching the east. From the contemplative point of view we need to relate practice, whether eastern or western, to the situation in which we find ourselves as westerners. So, for myself, a lot of my own journey has been trying to understand what it means to practice as a Buddhist and as a westerner coming from a Christian background. How do I actually relate the Buddhist teachings on suffering, letting go suffering, the cause of suffering, the cessation of suffering, to the actual situations in which I'm involved, the kind of relationships that I have with the people around me, the people who are my community around me here and now. I think that is the contribution that eastern teachings can make to our western situation...an antidote to this feeling that we always have to be concerned about the people over there who are obviously suffering out there.

One of the things that my meditation teacher in England used to say was, to those of us who were struggling with the vocation and being in a community when there was so much obvious suffering going on around the world, "Well, look, there are lot of middle class people here who are coming to us, who are suffering and their suffering is equally intense. They have a kind of existential suffering that meditation can directly address." And I think that's the challenge as a Christian and as a Buddhist, at this time, in this place, in the kind of world that we exist in...can we actually feel, can we actually touch the suffering of those who are closest to us? That is the kind of realism that eastern influence can bring in here. Of course, when you're in India, the social context is wholly different and so a wise man, a holy man, who emerges from that context has his own responsibility. This is hard to make a judgement on when you are coming from such a completely alien culture.

Donald Allchin: I was just thinking of the whole mysterious difference between the Christian way of thinking and speaking which involves the engagement with history as we understand it in the Judaeo-Christian tradition and in Christian scriptures, and also of course this fundamental way of thinking of God as Trinity. I was thinking specifically of Raymond Panikkar's book, which is about 30 years old now but which is a very fine book, called The Trinity and the Experience of Man. It's a very fascinating and very profound early contribution to Hindu-Christian dialogue. I've been thinking of it recently because there's a very fine essay on it by Rowan Williams in his book On Christian Theology. He has a fascinating essay there in which he discusses Panikkar's thoughts about the mystery of the Trinity in relationship to other religious traditions which are not specifically trinitarian. Surely in all religions we are concerned with seeing how to relate unity and distinction, unity and difference and this is one of the basic ways in which Christianity has found that and I am sure that in Hinduism and other great traditions it's done in different ways but maybe we are all involved in similar exploration.

What is always striking to someone like myself who is older is to observe how very easily and naturally and without any thought people who are fifty years younger than myself simply do all that. Just as people know how computers work almost without thinking, so they are actually involved in Christian-Buddhist dialogue or whatever it may be. This is certainly true of Christian people. How far it is true of Buddhist people let us say in a country like Japan, or of Hindus in other East Asian countries which have been more westernised at a technological level than India, I don't know. But it seems as though there is a kind of inner dialogue going on inside people all the time. I find that extraordinarily fascinating and also extraordinarily hopeful. What we are painfully trying to talk about is actually going on inside a lot of people as it is inside us.

Tony Pannett: Patrick touched on a very important point which comes up a lot when I'm in dialogue either in an official or in a simple friendly way with people that I meet. The business of the individual, the self and the other. How Christians view the self...the belief, the traditional teaching, that we shall be resurrected as an individual person at the last day. Which means "What do we mean we shall be resurrected? What central part of myself are we talking about?" Donald touched on the point too, I think – it is the whole business that we deal with – the one and the many. This is really the point.

PW: Being resurrected as an individual is not a Christian doctrine. Being resurrected in community [is] . . .

TP: Yes. As a person in community.

PW: Individual is a word that's not really in the Christian vocabulary.

DA: But unfortunately, it has been. You or I wouldn't like it to be. We come out of a particular tradition which has made a very strong distinction between person and individual. And I find that very important. But of course even a lot of Christians don't necessarily understand that distinction in the way in which, if you like, from Coleridge onward, we have. It relates clearly to the doctrine of the Trinity itself...

PE: I don't know how many people here are familiar with the transcriptions of papers and talks given at the Gethsemani Encounter in which many of these things were discussed. Donald said he didn't know how much some of these issues have become issues and how much influence the dialogue has had on others outside the Christian tradition. But in that [Encounter] we were able to hear Christian and Buddhist monks tackling the same question from their different points of view. It was very helpful and insightful and very provocative. But to come back to this meeting. Saccidananda[1] Ashram really began with Abhishiktananda[2]... And at Abhishiktananda's heart was the whole Advaitic experience of unity and oneness, but not a monotheism or anything monolithic.

It was unitive but still carried a diversity exemplified by the Trinity in Christianity. Indeed Bede's theological reflection came out of his own Advaitic experience which he was able to relate and articulate through his understanding and experience of the Christian view of a Trinitarian God. Work on that was the focus from which his views of Advaitic and Trinitarian experience conditioned the work that flowed from it. I don't think that Bede fully resolved the issue other than in himself, and particularly in the last three years of his life after his so-called stroke when he had that really profound experience. And so the work continues. As Kim was saying, this is an ongoing wrestling that is not comfortable and does not provide a nice, easy, neat answer in which we reckon we've got it all figured. You know there's pain, and you know we never really can be entirely satisfied.

DS: One of the things that struck me when people were talking was how we deal with concepts in the east and in the west. I remember at that gathering with the Dalai Lama and the Christian Meditation Movement, each day he commented on a gospel passage. He read the passage first and then commented. One day he read an account of the resurrection and you could see everybody say, 'What's he possibly going to say about this?' When he finished the account he just smiled and chuckled—as only he can chuckle. And he said, "Not a problem. Jesus fully enlightened." I think that sometimes in the East there is a facility to get to the heart of what is really a problem and what is really an opportunity.

One of things I was going to ask Kim was about one of the articles in the current issue of *The Merton Journal*. In it Patrick Barry who used to be abbot at Ampleforth asks why are there no monastic vocations today. I'm hoping that Kim may do something in reply to that – because Patrick Barry is talking specifically about Christian monasticism; I'm not entirely sure if it's the same – whether you've had the same question in Buddhist monasticism. I'm not even sure if you've had the same in [Christian] Orthodox monasticism either...

KW-M: We are talking about the western experience. Buddhism as everyone here knows is very popular in the west but is still at an early stage in terms of its monastic development. We've only had Buddhist monastic communities for twenty or thirty years or so, maybe a little bit longer in the States. Our drop out rate is fairly heavy too. A large intake and a fairly large drop out rate seems kind of okay in the Buddhist tradition but I think that remains to be seen to a great extent. What is more revealing from the Christian point of view is the lack of vocations. I think this reflects on the way in which the structures of the Church have been so dominant and that is why I would advocate contemplative spiritual revolution. This is what the church needs in order for these structures to collapse and allow to come to light the more simple forms of monasticism which appeal to westerners who go into Buddhist monasticism. At the moment the picture young people who are keen to go into spirituality have of Christianity is of a church that is utterly conservative. They are very intimidated by that and put off by it.

There's a lovely monk whom some of you may know, Father Rowland Walls. He's been a monk now for many years and used to be a professor, I think in Manchester. He has a little skete just outside Edinburgh. I often come across people in bars and nightclubs who are in a terrible state and I just tell them about this monk, this 82 year old monk, who lives in an old miners' community hall in a miners' village outside Edinburgh with two other monks. I tell them about him and say "Look, let me just take you out to see this guy. He'll sort you out." And he does, in his own inimitable way. That is the kind of voice that really speaks to people with a genuine experience of spirituality rather than mere theory. That's why I find it kind of amusing just to hear the kind of nit-picking in a theoretical kind of dialogue rather than the actual experiential kind of dialogue which Merton had. That's what we need to be doing. We need to be talking about our experience of spirituality in order to engage people outside. They need it desperately.

Hospice Worker: I'm really picking up on Kim's point. I don't know how to put this but I work with people who are dying every day. That's my job. And I'm a spiritual wanderer, I suppose. I've looked at all sorts of stories and traditions. I've looked at the Tibetan traditions about dying and it's really a struggle how to bring that into practice because I think it's very valuable but it's actually how you do it. I try and do it but even with meditating and bringing oneself into the presence of somebody who is dying... I've been to San Francisco and the hospice there where that is part of their practice with people who are dying. I'm not sure quite what I'm asking but it's like…it's like joining in with a community of…actually enabling me to do that because it's something that I need to do every day, I suppose. Maybe other people have experienced that as well…

DS: You're aware of the book from France by Marie de Hennezel, *Intimate Death*. It's certainly one of the best books I have read in the last three or four years.

HW: Hennezel relates the stories that we all come across every day of our lives.

DS: It's that whole concept of *Intimate Death*…of getting close and travelling with someone. There are some quite provocative perceptions in that book. For example, she says that people who come into the hospice with no explicit connection to a religious community or a faith community on the whole tend to engage with the dying process much more positively and creatively than people who do, which is a very interesting point. I think it's back to Kim's point about how you relate your experience in terms, if you do belong to a faith community, if it's real, if it's engaging with actually what Patrick was saying earlier, with the real problems of suffering and everything else. And maybe at the end of the day it's about being there and just letting go of whether you've got the answers because nobody's got the answers when people are there dying. It's just about being there in a sense. I think we need to reassure each other about that. That's quite difficult in a world where people don't have this kind of dialogue. That's maybe why revolutionary is the right word. We really do need to turn it all upside down.

Ian Thomson: When you were saying you needed some sort of communal support, of community as the basis of support, I'm not quite sure what you were getting at…

KW-M: That's what I heard you from what you were saying that…

IT: You needed some sort of open-ended community that's not geographically based…?

HW: That's partly what I'm saying. Because of the Tibetan traditions of death and dying, of actually visiting there and finding that it's not what I need. I have to put it like that. Because it is actually quite rigid and structured. One has to buy into a whole load of stuff in order to be there. That's my experience.

KW-M: I think that's what I heard you were saying...what is the kind of practice that can you do as a helper to be with people who are dying? From my point of view that is very much where I see the function of the monastic community. It is to create, to provide, to support, to provide a help to the helpers. Not necessarily to do the helping. Because a monastic contemplative is actually, as has been described many times by Merton, on the edge between life and death, actually going through that experience of dying to the self and to the ego as part of daily practice. That is, in a sense, the place where you have to be, in order to be with death and to trust in that process of dying. Really the monastics are the ones who are the professionals and that I think is something that is being rediscovered very powerfully in Buddhist monasticism in the west, finding that it is a resource for the community, not to be isolated from the community. If there is going to be a resurgence of Christian contemplative monasticism, I think that is maybe an example that they can pick up on, rather than that older tradition of monasticism secluded from the community.

HW: But it's an important form of networking. I'm aware of this. It's partly how to put this into practice. An interesting form of networking...of actually feeling the networks speaking. I'm aware now that I'm actually quite near the Buddhist monastery at Chithurst...

PE: Certainly in the United States there's a real breakdown in any sort of community atmosphere. For the most part you may know your next door neighbour peripherally but other than that you really don't know most of the people in your housing estate. And yet following the pattern of Alcoholics Anonymous, the *Tulsa World* newspaper serving a city of just about 350,000 people, each Sunday publishes a list of support groups. And there are two full pages of them. There are literally hundreds of support groups for just about every possible thing that you could imagine from spiritual to whatever. I think that what you're asking for and what Ian is suggesting, reflects a longing. This is how *Monos* began. I came across so many Christians who were meditators and contemplatives, and spiritual revolutionaries, and who felt themselves isolated and had no one to talk to, no one who could understand the language of the things they were struggling with. So that in some sense through our journal we aim to give them at least some sense of support. And I think that what you're asking for is something along those lines. Monastic communities are one resource that are suitable for some...it depends on the monastic community a lot but certainly there is a real need anyway for that.

HW: This support, actually, is what we all need in some form or another...

TP: Well, many thanks to everyone for their contribution...to Danny, to Kim, to Patrick. It's been a very fruitful dialogue as far as I am concerned and I am sure for many others. And I hope it will continue beyond this room. Thank you all very much.

Notes and References

1. Saccidananda is a use of three Sanskrit words, 'pure being' (sat), 'consciousness' (cit) and 'bliss' (ananda). Abhishiktananda used these terms to express the Christian experience of the Holy Trinity in terms of Advaitic experience.
2. Abhishiktananda was the Indian name adopted by Henri le Saux. After nearly 20 years in a Breton Benedictine monastery, he came to India in 1947 to live the rest of his life as a sannayasi, first with Fr Jules Monchanin at their Saccidananda Ashram at Shantivanam, Tamilnadu (where Bede Griffiths subsequently settled) and later as a hermit at Tiruvanamalai, and amid the Himalayas. See also Patrick Eastman's essay above.

Night is Our Ministry:
Monastic Vigil

MONIKA-CLARE GHOSH

[This title is adapted from Merton's poem
'The Quickening of St John the Baptist']

Night is our diocese and silence is our ministry
Poverty our charity and helplessness our tongue-tied sermon.
Beyond the scope of sight or sound we dwell upon the air
Seeking the world's gain in an unthinkable experience.
We are exiles in the far end of solitude, living as listeners
With hearts attending to the skies we cannot understand:
Waiting upon the first far drums of Christ the Conqueror
Planted like sentinels upon the world's frontier.

IN HIS *Asian Journal* MERTON DESCRIBED THE "PARTICULAR OFFICE OF THE monk in the modern world" as being "to keep alive the contemplative experience", and I suggest that one important aspect of this "experience" is that of keeping vigil, of watching and waiting, of prayer at night.

I have to admit that when I started looking for references to the monastic practice of vigil and to prayer during the night in Merton's writings, I was surprised not to find a lot more discussion of the spiritual and liturgical significance of the monastic practice. He has, of course, left some marvellous descriptions of his experiences of night, from the 'Fire Watch' when he walked the deserted cloisters as a young monk while his brethren slept, to his last years in his woodland hermitage.

Throughout his life as a monk, his days and nights followed the monastic rhythm laid down by St Benedict as interpreted by the Cistercians of his time, and in his 'Project for a Hermitage' (a remarkably unattractive document, presumably written to reassure hide-bound authorities!) he describes the *horarium* of a projected semi-eremitical Skete,

> Normally all would rise a little earlier than in the monastic community, that is to say, at two o'clock or earlier. It would be understood that all would be saying Vigils and making their meditation and so on in the night hours and all would say Lauds at about dawn...

Vigils have survived in the modern secular world. Candlelight vigils may be kept in protest, as a sign of solidarity, to commemorate anniversaries. Some of you may have witnessed the scenes in London on the night preceding Princess Diana's funeral.

However, here I will only consider monastic vigils, where the 'watching' is a form of 'praying'. We speak of 'keeping vigil'—that word 'keeping' is significant. We *keep* vigils, *keep* silent, *keep* a fast or feast, *keep* the Sabbath. These are all symbolic enactments of some important aspect of our faith which needs nurturing. They also involve doing something, not just thinking about it, but they aren't absolutes; life is not intended to be unbroken vigil, silence, fast, feast or Sabbath. One important thing to remember is that they don't get us brownie points "the Lord pours gifts on his beloved while they sleep" the psalmist reminds us. There is nothing inherently virtuous about them; they are part of a pattern that must include their contrary. It does of course take some effort to keep vigil, but above all it is a gift, and by receiving it we enter into a mystery—it leads us into a land of paradox, and here as ever the Lord has gone before us.

We probably realise more clearly than previous generations that our earthly time is local—we know that the solar eclipse or millennial midnight races towards us across the planet, that comets come from another part of our universe, trailing our distant past in their wake. Even here on earth, when it is night in one place, it is day elsewhere, and some aspects of time are culturally-determined human realities: 24-hour banking, shopping and working have made the hours of one person's 'night', times of lights and work for his or her neighbour. I shan't attempt to discuss the insights of relativity, quantum physics, cosmology and chronobiology, but they have all obviously had their impact. Perhaps all this makes awareness of the graces of prayer in the night more urgent than ever. The night-time worship of the monastery reminds us that our roots must run deep into the quiet stillness, darkness and silence, of openness and wonder. It plunges us into the mystery of time itself, and releases the inherent energy of an interface, a 'frontier'.

Dom André Louf, the former abbot of the French Cistercian monastery of Mont des Cats who is now living in solitude, writes

> At the crack of dawn, at the coming of the light, the monk stands on that frontier between the world which is passing away and the world which is coming. He looks towards the Saviour who always comes with mercy…what is more his prayer hastens the coming of Christ in glory. (*The Cistercian Way*)

Esther de Waal, in *Living with Contradiction* (chapter entitled 'Death and Life'), quotes another living Cistercian:

> Matthew Kelty tells us that the feast of John the Baptist has always been a particular favourite with the monks because it comes just at the time (it falls on 24th June) when the sun begins its journey down, a dying which we all know will eventually lead to life.
>
> The monk sees in the plunge into night his own way into the darkness of God.

In the readings of the liturgy, during his first monastic Advent, Merton will have frequently been led to meditate on John the Baptist, from his quickening in Elizabeth's womb, when he, like David, danced at the coming of the Lord, to the desert and the Jordan where he recognised the Lamb of God, to his doubts in prison and his death, foreshadowing that of Christ. The Benedictus is sung daily at the end of Lauds—in it the father of John the Baptist blesses God "who visits us like the Dawn from on high". It celebrates the great hinge of time.

Above all, in the Gospels we see Christ going out alone at night – often into the desert – to pray before important turning points. Indeed, Merton's own abbey carried the name of 'Gethsemani'—the starkest place of Christ's prayer at night.

But before we look at the specifically Christian aspects of the monastic vigil, it may be interesting to see how it is lived in other monastic traditions. I was struck by the close parallel between the timetable followed by Merton and that given by the Dalai Lama describing his routine. Writing to his Muslim friend Abdul Aziz on 2 January 1966 Merton wrote,

> I go to bed about 7:30 at night and rise about 2:30 in the morning. On rising I say part of the canonical office consisting of psalms, lessons etc. Then I take an hour or an hour and a quarter for meditation. I follow

this with some Bible reading and then make some tea or coffee and
have breakfast if it is not a fast day.

With breakfast I begin reading and continue reading/studying until
sunrise...

Incidentally he had previously assured his friend that he
remembered him often, particularly at dawn, Merton continues,

... At sunrise I say another office of psalms etc. and then begin
my work, which includes sweeping, clearing, cutting wood and other
necessary jobs....

In 1996, the Dalai Lama attended a 5-day meeting at Gethsemani
and in response to a question outlined his own daily practice,

I must say I am a very poor practitioner. Usually I get up at 3:30 in the
morning. Then I immediately do some recitations and some chanting.
Following this until breakfast I do meditation ...

Here his Holiness described his practice of meditation.

So from around 3:30 a.m. until 8:30 a.m. I am fully occupied with
meditation and prayer and things like that. During that time I take a
few breaks, including my breakfast – which is usually at 5:00 am – and
some prostrations. After 8:30 a.m,, when my mood is good I do some
physical exercise.

After a busy day, he has his evening meal at about 6 p.m. and
retires for what he calls his "most favorite, peaceful meditation" at
around 8:30 p.m.

I think one would find a similar pattern in many monasteries of
different faith traditions. It is simply rooted in human nature, which
of course makes it an ideal sacramental vehicle for the experience of
"standing before the living God" as the prophet Elijah described it,
or of 'practising meditation', 'standing' or 'sitting' as other traditions
describe it.

In the Jewish and Islamic traditions, regular prayer throughout
the day and night is the duty of the whole Community and of every
believer.

In the Jewish tradition the institution of the Dawn prayer service
is sometimes attributed to Abraham. Commenting on Chapter 19 of
Genesis (after the destruction of Sodom and Gomorrah), the Torah
commentary of the Safat Emmet says,

Abraham established the dawn prayer service, as Scripture tells us: "He
arose early to that place where he had stood in God's presence (Gen

19:27)" i.e. he was able to get back to that spiritual place where he had been on the previous night when he lay down. This is the way of those who serve God... Thus we say in our prayers, 'May we arise and find our heart's hope'. For this is a sign that we truly love God: if as soon as we awaken we can recall our Creator before we do anything else... Thus Scripture testifies that Abraham, the Pillar of Love, "Abraham my [friend] lover" (Is 41:8) arose early to that place where he had stood. This is what they mean when they say that he established the dawn service: he gave the power to each Jew to arouse the dawn every day. "Awake, my soul! Awake, harp and lyre! I will awake the dawn." (Ps 56/57)

This notion of leaving a sort of 'bookmark' in one's mind overnight, so that it falls open at adoration, is something else all traditions share.

Islamic tradition prescribes hours of prayer throughout the day, but not at night; however it does recount a mysterious night-time episode which is often interpreted as a spiritual experience: Muhammud's journey from Mecca to Jerusalem on his steed Buraq and accompanied by the angel Gabriel. From the Noble Sanctuary – the Dome of the Rock – the Prophet ascended to God in the seventh heaven.

We must not limit the notion of 'keeping vigil' to ritual prayers. The psalms often speak of meditating on God in bed, of the heart remaining awake during the watches of the night and the Lord Jesus himself clearly valued the peace of the night for solitary prayer.

In his Life of St Benedict, St Gregory describes the famous vision in which Benedict saw the world in a ray of light—an 'enlightenment'-like experience...and this occurred when he had risen before his fellow monks, long before the night office, and was standing looking out of the window.

I think we can genuinely consider the silence and darkness of the night to be sacramental. If we are not so sleepy as to make attention impossible, it is probably the easiest time to achieve focussed stillness and see many things in a totally new way. In his poem 'La Nuit', Claudel speaks of the Night as a beloved daughter of God, for whom he has made a wonderful dark mantle decked with stars. There can be few people – believers or unbelievers – who have not been moved to wonder by the spectacle of the starlit night sky. The celebrated Benedictine abbot of Bec-Hellouin, Dom Paul Grammont[1] tells of an old French country woman who told her parish priest that one advantage of being old was that one had time to pray. After asking how he got on with his breviary, the old woman told him "When I open wide my door in the early morning and see the stars before dawn, I repeat the phrase from the psalm 'The heavens are telling the glory of God...'". The whole psalm (Psalm 18) is a lovely expression of praise in response to the glory of God glimpsed in his creation, and particularly in the beauty of his "daughter" in her starry mantle. It may be helpful sometimes to go out armed with just a single phrase such as this and pray/think/savour it under a starlit sky.

Merton obviously did just that in his night hours in the hermitage. He describes, for instance, coming out onto the porch before dawn, full of sombre thoughts about Vietnam, and seeing a comet.

> The comet! I heard about it yesterday in the monastery, went out to see it this morning, and went at just the right time. It was magnificent; appearing just at the ineffable point when the first dim foreshadowing light (that is not light yet) makes one suspect the sun will rise. This great sweep of pure silent light points to the sun that will come—it takes in a good area of sky right over the valley in front of the hermitage. I walked down the path to see it well. It was splendid. I interrupted reading Isaac of Stella's Fourteenth Sermon on God's light in his joy in His creation...
>
> Riches! ...I recited Psalm 18 *coeli enarrant* "The heavens are telling" with joy.

I wonder, did he hear in his head the marvellous setting of these words by Haydn, inspired by his first view of the heavens through a telescope? Merton's description will remind many of us of the gracious visit of comet Hale Bopp to our night skies in recent years. I'm sure I wasn't the only one to stand on my porch and remember Henry Vaughan's words:

> I saw Eternity the other night
> Like a great Ring of pure and endless light...
> There is in God (some say)
> a deep and dazzling darkness.

Merton had entered Gethsemani in December and, like every Cistercian novice before and since I imagine, he was overwhelmed by the pure beauty of the Advent liturgy.

In 1964 he looked back on that time,

> At the hermitage these cold nights I have spontaneously been remembering the days when I first came to Gethsemani 23 years ago. The stars, the cold, the smell of night, the wonder (the "abandonment"

which is something else again than despondency) and above all the melody of *Rorate coeli*. That entire first Advent bore in it all the stamp of my vocation's special character. The solitude, inhabited and pervaded by cold and mystery, by woods and Latin. It is surprising how far we have got from the cold and the woods and the stars since those early days! (October 31, 1964)

He was ending his 50th year and it was the stars – Orion and Aldebaran – and the moon, that seemed to say to him, "It is the *Kairos*"—the time is ripe. Later that year, he wrote during Advent:

One can pretend in the solitude of an afternoon walk, but the night destroys all pretences, one is reduced to nothing, and compelled to begin laboriously the long return to truth. (December 5, 1964)

And a year later, on December 10, 1965

Celebrating my twenty-third anniversary of arrival at Gethsemani. Long quiet evening, rain falling, candle, silence: it is incomparable!.

In *Day of a Stranger*, also written in 1965 when he was living in the hermitage, he described his vigils,

I live in the woods out of necessity. I get out of bed in the middle of the night because it is imperative that I hear the silence of the night, alone, and with my face on the floor say psalms, alone, in the silence of the night...

I have an obligation to preserve the stillness, the silence, the poverty, the virginal point of pure nothingness, which is at the centre of all other loves. I cultivate this plant silently in the middle of the night and water it with psalms and prophecies in silence...

It is necessary for me to see the first point of light which begins to be dawn. It is necessary to be present alone at the resurrection of Day, in the solemn silence at which the sun appears.

Why then does the Christian monk feel it necessary to keep vigil? I don't think the reason is primarily ascetic—the aim isn't really sleep deprivation. Nor is it puritanical…saying prayers at night isn't primarily a way of avoiding debauchery, let alone compensating for it in others, though some of the old Latin hymns do suggest this! I don't think it is mainly practical either, although it is certainly easier to avoid being disturbed or distracted at these rather uncivilised hours.

Part of the explanation lies in the middle-eastern origins of the liturgy. The celebration of Sunday – or any major feast – starts not in the morning, but at first vespers, celebrated the previous evening. So the night is part of the feast, not simply a preparation for it. Sadly, in the Catholic Church the introduction of 'Saturday evening Mass' has probably destroyed the last vestige of this, as it is rarely a Vigil Mass ushering the believers into the celebration of the 'eighth day' when time goes beyond itself into eternity, but tends to be seen as a way of getting one's obligation out of the way!

My own favourite mental 'ikon' of the monk keeping vigil is the description of the great Abba Arsenius. We are told that on Saturday evening, he turned his back to the setting sun and stretched out his hands in prayer to heaven until the sun shone on his face once more. Then he sat down in the splendour of the dawning Sunday.

The Vigil of course is the Easter Vigil. Ideally the whole night is spent in retelling and reliving the wonderful story of our creation and salvation in story and song, with the marvellous symbol of the great candle standing as a pillar of fire in our midst until it pales in the light of dawn. It also reminds us that God was the first to keep Vigil,

> That was for the Lord a night of vigil, to bring them out of the land of Egypt. That same night is a vigil to be kept for the Lord by all the Israelites throughout their generations. (Exodus 12: 42)

The Easter vigil culminates with the dawn celebration of the encounter between Mary Magdalene, the apostle of the apostles, and the Risen Christ.

In the Gospels we see the Lord going out to pray at night, and urging his disciples to watch and pray for they know not the hour. The hour: that of temptation, of testing, that of the coming of the Kingdom, coming like a thief in the night, late in the evening, in the middle of the night or before dawn. Who can know?

When the Spirit drives someone out into the 'desert' to pray, that person, like Christ, learns to rely increasingly on the word of God and above all on the psalms.

Probably no-one has caught the beauty of the night as vividly as John of the Cross.

> O night that guided me! O night more lovely than the dawn.

We have probably all recognised the thrill of slipping out into a grey pre-dawn to go to early Mass—particularly if one is a convert and Mass-going still has something dangerous and even seditious about it. John describes "going abroad when all my house was hushed"

> In safety, in disguise,
> In darkness up the secret stair I crept.

"Where is he? Have you seen him?" The frantic questions of the Bride in the Canticle, seeking her beloved through the night of grief have been echoed down the centuries of Judaeo-Christian prayer. Psalm 29/30 praises the Lord

> For his anger is but for a moment;
> his favour is for a lifetime.
> Weeping may linger for the night,
> but joy comes with the morning.

The psalmist's experience leads from mourning into dancing:

> You have taken off my sackcloth
> and clothed me with joy,
> so that my soul may praise you
> and not be silent.
> O Lord my God,
> I will give thanks to you forever.

There is a whole spirituality of the 'Night', in which the darkness, the silence, the stillness are not negative, but luminous, music and dancing, and Merton revelled in it. But that will have to be another paper!

We'd better head back to the sobriety of the monastic tradition! In the Rule which Merton followed at Gethsemani, St Benedict tells his monks that they—like boy scouts—must always be ready! They rise when their sleep is finished (rather than getting up in the middle of the night and then returning to bed), and they sleep fully clothed, so that they can rise without delay, encouraging one another as they rise from sleep and hasten together to the Oratory. Then after the Night Office they wait for the dawn, when they will celebrate Lauds. The monk is a "watchman" listening for the shout of joy in the night; his task is not to repel hostile invaders, but to fling open the doors for Christ the Bridegroom when he comes for the wedding feast. In many modern monasteries, the hours of vigil culminate in the Eucharist at dawn.

In St Benedict's Prologue to his *Rule* we read—as of course Merton read:

> However late it may seem, let us rouse ourselves from lethargy. That is what Scripture urges on all when it says "the time has come for us to rouse outselves from sleep" (Rm 13:11). Let us open our eyes to the light that shows us the way to God. Let our ears be alert to the stirring call of his voice, do not harden you hears (Psalm 94/5:8).

St Benedict uses the language of vigil, of watching and waiting, to characterise the monk's whole way of life. Benedict drew heavily on John Cassian's description of early Egyptian monasticism, and writing of Cassian's teaching, Merton says:

> ... To embrace the eremitical life is to ascend the "high mountain of solitude with Christ" And to do this is to obey most perfectly Christ's monastic call to prayer. Indeed, it is to follow His example, for He himself withdrew to pray on the mountain by night in order to give Christians an example of solitary prayer. (*The Humanity of Christ in Monastic Prayer*)

One of the most compelling descriptions Cassian gives of early monastic practice is that of the monks gathering for the Night Office celebrated in the desert:

> ...they are all so perfectly silent that, though so large a number of the brethren is assembled together, you would not think a single person was present except the one who stands up and chants the Psalm in the midst; and especially is this the case when the prayer is offered up...when the Psalm is ended they do not hurry at once to kneel down, ...but before they bend their knees they pray for a few moments, and while they are standing up spend the greater part of the time in prayer. And so after this, for the briefest space of time, they prostrate themselves to the ground, as if but adoring the Divine Mercy, and as soon as possible rise up, and again standing erect with outspread hands – just as they had been standing to pray before – remain with thoughts intent upon their prayers... But when he who is to "collect" the prayer rises from the ground they all start up at once, so that no one would venture to bend the knee before he bows down, nor to delay when he has risen from the ground, lest it should be thought that he has offered his own prayer independently instead of following the leader to the close.

In this description we sense a seamless combination of ascetic practice, liturgical celebration and spiritual experience.[2]

The Egyptian monks invariably chanted 12 psalms at the Night Office every day, and from that time until very recently, the Church kept to this rule, which was claimed to have been instituted by an angel, who appeared to settle disputes among the monks about how many psalms should be said. When the nights were short in summer or time short for some other reason, Benedict envisages shortening the readings, but not deviating from the sacrosanct twelve psalms. This office consists almost entirely of psalms and readings from the Old Testament. But of course the traditional understanding of these texts often interprets them as spoken by Christ himself or as casting light on his Coming. For instance in the book of Wisdom, after a dramatic description of the terrors faced by the Egyptians in the night of the Passover, we read,

> For while gentle silence enveloped all things, and night in its swift course was now half gone, your all-powerful word leaped from heaven, from the royal throne. (Wisdom 18:14)

These words inevitably call to mind the Coming of Christ—Emmanuel, God with us.

The great Syrian teacher, Isaac, says that the monk's vigil involves both "standing" i.e. silent prayer, and psalmody. "One man continues in psalmody all night long; another passes the night in repentance."

The joy in their hearts keeps them from even thinking of sleep, for it seems to them that they have put off the body or that they have already reached the state they will enjoy after the resurrection.[3] This great joy sometimes leads them to leave off psalmody as they fall prostrate on account of the onrush of joy that surges in their soul. The whole length of the night is like the day to them, and the coming of darkness is like the rising of the sun[4] because of the hope which exalts their hearts and inebriates them by its meditation, and from the blazing of their minds which burn with the spiritual memory of the good things of the age to come.

Like every Christian, the monk claims the citizenship of heaven; his conversation is to be in heaven, in the New Jerusalem where there is no longer any night, and so presumably no vigil, for the Lamb himself is a flaming torch. Or is it all vigil—the angels are traditionally known as the holy watchers? But meanwhile, while day and night, light and dark alternate, the monk calls from the ends of the earth in a weak voice, often weak in faith, a sinner only Christ can save. Murmuring God's law by day and by night he clings to the mystery of faith, knowing that the Church waits with Christ, and for Christ—preaching Christ crucified and proclaiming the death of

Christ in the glory of the Risen Christ. There is one Christ waiting and awaited, as there will be one Christ loving himself.

One of the great challenges to the monastics of our age may be to help to keep alive this contemplative experience, to be beacons of 'watching and waiting' in an increasingly rushing world. Any practice must be rooted in the truth, in the 'reality', of life. All too often, 'saying prayers' becomes a major obstacle to growth in real prayer...and indeed to real life at all. Yet some sort of practice is essential. It is often a long struggle, and in a changing world will probably be a dynamic equilibrium rather than a rigid and potentially alienating 'rule'. Whatever our practice, it must enable us to grow in the ability to recognise the presence of God in our entire life, rather than being a refuge from reality. Merton knew how the stability of monastic life – its sheer unchanging monotony – could deepen this experience:

> One has to be in the same place every day, watch the dawn from the same house, hear the same birds wake each morning to realise how inexhaustibly rich and different is 'sameness'. This is the blessing of stability and I think it is not evident until you enjoy it alone in a hermitage.

If at times, in Merton's words, we feel ourselves to be exiled "in the far end of solitude,… Planted like sentinels upon the world's frontier, with hearts attending to the skies we cannot understand", we must seek to "live as listeners".[5]

I'd like to end with the prayer of the Irish missionary monk, St Columbanus, who clearly saw his life as a Vigil in the temple of the Lord:

> I pray in the name of Jesus Christ
> the Son, my God, I pray you Lord,
> grant me that love which knows no fall
> so that my lamp may feel the kindling touch
> and know no quenching,
> and may burn for me and for others may give LIGHT.
> O Christ, deign to kindle our lamps,
> our Saviour most sweet to us,
> that they may shine continually in your temple,
> and receive perpetual light from you who are light perpetual,
> so that our darkness may be driven far from us.

Notes and References

1. Dom Paul Grammont. *Le Feu qui nous habite*. Paroles de Vie, 1990. My translation.
2. I have skipped passages in which Cassian uses the Egyptian practice to criticize what he sees as slackness in the monasteries of Gaul.
3. The monk is rooted in the paschal reality of baptism and called to be a prophet of the age to come... Isaac taught that silence is the language of the age to come, that it will enlighten us in God. The Christian lives in the *kairos*, the hinge between this visible world and the promised Kingdom coming into being in us and around us, calling us forward to an unimaginable future. This aspect of our being vibrates in the night, we recognise our longings in those of the Church waiting in hope for the return of the Bridegroom.
4. "The night shall be as the day. The Lord himself will be our light."
5. From Merton's poem, 'The Quickening of St John the Baptist'.

A City
Is Something You Do...

GARY P. HALL

Christianity has continually found new forms through needing to be
worked out afresh in new situations; and the situations have often
involved deprivation, suffering, marginalization. The shift from the
province of Judaea to urban centres in the rest of the Roman Empire
was the first such transition.

So WRITES DAVID FORD IN HIS ESSAY 'Transformation', PRODUCED FOR
the Archbishop of Canterbury's Urban Theology Group a few years
ago.[1] From within the city it would appear that the general trend
has been for some time a shift *away from* urban centres – or more
specifically, away from the city centres and urban priority areas –
towards the suburbs, coastal towns andmarket towns such as
Oakham... If that perception is borne out in fact, it may partly
explain the resurgence of forms of theology and spirituality which
call themselves "urban."

Thomas Merton's vocational impulse took him on a trajectory away
from the city too, towards the rural (medieval) context of Gethsemani
Abbey. So when in one of his later essays we find him writing out of
that context about the city, city-dwellers are understandably curious
as to what he has to say. Does Merton offer resources for interpreting
urban dynamics and shaping urban praxis?

We had to work out afresh our faith-response to a new situation
which arose in the inner-city district of Hyde Park, Leeds during the
summer of 1995. In the aftermath of a small but significant riot in
that down-town neighbourhood in July of that year, Merton's essay,
'The Street is for Celebration', – in the posthumously-published
collection, *Love and Living*[2] – seemed as good a starting-point as any. In

light of the collective shock of what had happened in our midst, it was interesting reading.

We may now take for granted that all theology is contextual, though it is less obvious whether there are theological/spiritual sources, idioms, languages specifically suited to the city. Of course we may, as individuals within the city, find nourishment for our personal faith-life in mystics and writers such as Merton. But there are occasions when we are looking for something more, something which might help us together to interpret what happens in the city, and to shape our action. What has Merton to offer? Perhaps we would, after all, do better turning to sociologists or historians, anthropologists, even architects—and we may be grateful for their professional insights. But, in the end, our quest is different: if we are to "find our place in the world" (as Merton would describe it), we generally need some working definition of where, in detail, we are—the particular world we are part of. And we need that definition all the more if we happen to experience ourselves as alienated from our environment.

So with typically broad strokes, Merton in this essay offers a basic starting-point:

A city is something you do with space

The statement in its global starkness begs deconstruction. For most of us, a city is not like an artist's empty canvas awaiting our creative construction, but rather is something that *somebody else* does with space. We have little say in the matter. Other people hold the power and make the decisions which influence the lives of many city-dwellers. One of those aforementioned sociologists had this to say:

> The crucial urban types are those who control or manipulate scarce resources and facilities such as housing managers, estate agents, local government officers, property developers, representatives of building societies and insurance companies, youth employment officers, social workers, magistrates, councillors and so on.[3]

This is a point Merton himself takes seriously later in the essay: "We did not build our own city," he writes—becoming the voice of the disenfranchised. He goes on:

> We have been thrown out into this alienated camp of rats, in which we are not wanted, in which we are constantly reminded by everything around us that we are powerless. This city is not built for celebration

even though it calls itself 'Fun City'. Fun is for money. Fun is in buildings where you pay admission. (LL, p. 52)

Acknowledging that the city is by and large created and conducted by other people is not an abdication of responsibility for the life of the city, only a recognition of the limits of power and influence. The participation or collusion of each of us does to some degree shape our environment. However, the extent to which (or the way in which) a person may participate creatively in city life depends upon whether this "crowd of occupied spaces" are indeed "Occupied or inhabited? Filled or lived in?" (LL, p.46)

The answer to that particular question, suggests Merton, determines the character and quality of the city. And this in the end "may turn out to be a crucial question for a city, for a country, and for the world." Maybe it will. (There were, it must be said, quite a number of issues Merton considered vital at one time or another.)

The theme of 'space' is there in the work of sociologists such as Pahl – quoted previously – who a few years after Merton's essay suggests a dry but tantalising definition of the city as "A given context or configuration of reward-distributing systems which have space as significant component"[4] 'Space' was certainly a significant theme in Merton's own story. When Merton asks, "Can a street be an inhabited space? A space where people enjoy being? A space where people are present to themselves, with full identities, as real people, as happy people?" (LL, p.48), it is a question which resonates deep in his memory.

Merton had lived in a few cities. The evidence of his journals and other writings would suggest that he had often struggled in the city to be present to himself, with full identity... real... happy (as he puts it). For him the city (whether Cambridge, London, New York) had at times become "An alienated space, an uninhabited space...a space where you submit."

The city can also be dynamic, stimulating, festive, creative, fascinating—when we are at ease, when we belong, when we feel at home there. When we have little say, no role, when the city is shaped and imposed by people other than ourselves, then more intensely than any other environment, the city can impact upon our inner space, our emotional space. (Merton's reflections here are pertinent to our current consideration of the plight of asylum seekers here in the East Midlands, for example.)

There are fascinating echoes on this kind of experience in *My Argument with the Gestapo*, a novel written during that "vital and crucial period" of Merton's life in the summer of 1941.[5] In this book, which reveals infinitely more that *The Seven Storey Mountain* of what Merton was feeling during this period, we follow a fictional Merton through the synthetic scenes of a remembered life he could not entirely leave behind. Set in wartime England and France, the novel is a last-ditch attempt (as he put it) to "define the world's predicament" and to find his place in that world.[6]

In *The Seven Storey Mountain* Merton would eventually define his monastic life as a rejection of the World, with the implication that the world (as object) is 'the problem.' But this earlier writing which appeared posthumously is more subtle in its outlook. Here, Merton is well aware of projecting his feelings onto the external world. He knows well enough that the world is perceived through the lens of emotional memory. Let's take a particularly telling passage:

> London was once one city for me, and became, at a certain definite time, another. Both cities are being bombed, and both are real, but they cannot both be real to the same person at the same time, and the city that is being bombed is the one I discovered last. It is the real one, the actual city. The other is only in the mind. It no longer exists. [7]

Merton then goes on to describe the city as "*a city of angels, of good, well-mannered children*" and as a place of quasi-pastoral tranquillity. This is how it appears until,

> suddenly, sometime, not for everybody, and never for the innocent, the masks fall off the houses, and the streets become liars and the squares become thieves and the buildings become murderers.

Both cities are "real," as he puts it—but not at the same time. The external world, the world out there, is in some sense an extension of the inner world of the beholder. The "actual city" – the dark, brooding, hurting city – remains imperceptible to the "innocent." (Here we catch echoes of William Blake, on whose work Merton was writing his MA dissertation at Columbia.) That loss of innocence is itself reflected by the world (and not least in his recollection of a world at war), which evokes an emotional reaction from one in whom such feelings are already latent. In short, the city amplifies the inner experience of *anomie*, alienation, disintegration.

By the time Merton was writing 'The Street is for Celebration', he was more astutely aware of the psychological dynamic which inspired that writing half a life-time previously. The insights nevertheless remained valid (he was still keen for the novel to be published) and articulate an experience which many urban-dwellers in particular will relate to: Quite simply, that the city *does something* with our emotional space. The city is more than a mere backdrop onto which we project our emotional world. Rather, the city generates particular reactions within us, resonating with aspects of our mood or inner experience which might otherwise remain dormant.

Merton's decision to join the Trappists was at the same time a decision not to work in the inner city. During the summer of 1941, he attended an evening lecture at St Bonaventure University where he was teaching English. A Russian emigrée, Baroness Catherine de Hueck, was speaking of life in the poorest parts of Harlem—a few blocks away from Columbia University. She was well known in Corpus Christi parish and, although Merton was expecting to see someone else on the stage that evening, he tells of how he knew instantly who she was when he walked into a room of people hanging onto her every word. He too was moved deeply and, following a brief conversation with the Baroness, soon afterwards found himself at Friendship House on 135th Street, Harlem, offering to join in the work there.

Harlem and its people left their mark on Merton: In *The Seven Storey Mountain* he writes of having "come out of Harlem with what might well have been the problem of another vocation." His poem, 'Aubade – Harlem', dedicated to Baroness Catherine de Hueck, expresses the kind of impressions which remained with him:

> Across the cages of the keyless aviaries,
> The lines and wires, the gallows of the broken kites,
> Crucify; against the fearful light,
> The ragged dresses of the little children.
> Soon, in the sterile jungles of the waterpipes and ladders,
> The bleeding sun, a bird of prey, will terrify the poor,
> Who will forget the unbelievable moon.[8]

Meanwhile, Merton returned for the autumn term to continue teaching at St Bonaventure's, and the Baroness arrived again on campus where she was leading a retreat. She asked Merton directly when he intended to come to Harlem for good. Merton agreed (after some discussion) that he would move into Friendship House in January.

Merton, of course, was unsettled. A retreat at Gethsemani Abbey during the previous Holy Week had left even deeper impressions than the streets of Harlem. He concludes the matter in a journal entry of November 27, 1941:

> Should I be going to Harlem, or to the Trappists? Why doesn't this idea of the Trappists leave me? Perhaps what I am afraid of is to write and be rejected... Perhaps I cling to my independence, to the chance to write, to go where I like in the world... Going to Harlem... is a good and reasonable way to follow Christ. But going to the Trappists is exciting, it fills me with awe and desire. I return to the idea again and again: "Give up *everything*, give up *everything*!" [9]

A "good and reasonable way to follow Christ" is what the city offered. But Merton at that time was unprepared. Only by "giving up everything" could he imagine being released from persistent struggles and unresolved issues which the world – the city – only reinforced. The city doesn't permit that kind of letting go. The city can sustain whatever distorting self-consciousness we carry. The city feeds on fictions involving roles, positions, masks, baggage, needs and values. The city presses home its own concerns, along with the needs and demands of other people. The city, by and large, will not leave us alone.

> The greatest need of our time is to clean out the enormous mass of mental rubbish that clutters our minds and makes all political and social life a mass illness. Without this house-cleaning we cannot begin to see. Unless we see we cannot think. [10]

So Merton famously followed his instinct towards an entirely new context, a sacred context, a world apart, a world whose reality was validated by his sense of emotional liberty and cognitive clarity. This sacred world of the Abbey stands in contradistinction to the secular and apparently meaningless urban world, the street which, in the end,

> may be a dump for thousands of people who aren't there. They have been dumped there, but their presence is so provisional they might as well be absent. They occupy space by being displaced in it. They are out of place in the space allotted to them by society. (LL, p.47)

Although Merton (like most urban practitioners) could never claim to be urban poor, 'underclass,' whatever, he did share in the more common experience of alienation which a city can amplify. For this reason perhaps above all he remains a valued commentator for others engaging with the everyday experiences of urban dwellers. He too wanted to make a difference, and offered his own solutions:

> The people who are merely provisionally present, half-absent non-persons must now become really present on the street as themselves. They must be recognisable as people. Hence, they must recognise each other as people.

concludes Merton. With the poignant comment that "Business is not about to recognise them as people, only as consumers".[11]

Merton's own gradual dawning recorded and celebrated as a moment of 'enlightenment' at the corner of Fourth and Walnut in Louisville is testimony to his own erratic movement towards this recognition of human worth and dignity. Awakening to that undergirding human solidarity, that unity, was a liberating moment for Merton—a transforming vision, if you like. Some years later, in light of that affective insight, he is able to uncover some of the factors which prevent such recognition in the first place:

> To acquire inhabitants, the street will have to be changed. Something must happen to the street. Something must be done to it. Instead of submitting to the street, [the inhabitants] must change it. Instead of being formally and impersonally put in their place by the street, they must transform the street and make it over so that it is liveable. (LL, pp. 48-9)

Such transformation involves clear perception which may require a distancing, disengaging from the distortions and confusions which the city can generate. But in the final count, seeing, thinking, and action are intertwined:

> The street can be inhabited if the people on it begin to make their life credible by changing their environment. Living is more than submission: it is creation. To live is to create one's own world as a scene of personal happiness.

But 'How do you do that?' asks Merton. And hosts of urban workers echo the question or offer their partial replies. Does Merton have an answer for us?

Yes and no. In our very specific experience back in 1995, Merton did present a guiding light, but when we came round to reading this essay in the wake of an urban uprising, some of the detail of Merton's opinion were perhaps no more valid than the next opinion. He was too far from this particular experience.

It isn't immediately apparent what was in Merton's imagination when he spoke of those who seek to change their environment by "tearing the place apart." But he interprets that kind of social disorder – with its implications of destruction, looting, violence – as surrender:

> Violence in the street is all right as an affirmation that one does not submit, but it fails because it accepts the general myth of the street as no-man's-land, as battleground, as no place. Hence, it is another kind of submission. It takes alienation for granted. Merely to fight in the street is to protest, in desperation, that one is unable to change anything. So in the long run it is another way of giving up. (LL, p.49ff.)

During a six-year sojourn in inner-city Leeds, our neighbourhood hosted two significant riots. Not the scale or ferocity of, say, events in Toxteth or Brixton some years earlier; nor were they really "fighting in the street", violence against the person. Each event had its own distinct character, the second perhaps the more simple—a threatening reaction by a gang from outside the area to one of their drug distributors being arrested in Hyde Park. Cars were burned, walls were rammed, people were afraid, riot police missed the point.

The first disturbance, notwithstanding the panic-stricken hysteria from the suburban press, had quite a different flavour and origin, one with which a number of us had a lot more sympathy.

I think it was the early hours of July 11 that I had a phone call to say the Newlands pub was ablaze. Walking down there (our church was just opposite and many of our people lived round about the pub), the stench of burning cars and the glow of a gutted building filled the senses. There was a lot of madness that night. The tension which had been developing for days had exploded. People were frightened and confused—but there was more to this than met the eye, and infinitely more than the local media could understand.

To risk gross over-simplification by cutting a long story short, a public house which had become one of the last remaining meeting points for local people of all ages, in an area of great deprivation and disintegration, had been taken over as a police surveillance point. The reason was that with its open doors it had also hosted drug dealings and the distribution of stolen property. Nothing good in that. But the perceived loss of the pub as a meeting point was the final straw for the people who had little other community focus, and in the end the frustration exploded in the violent destruction of the pub itself. I think it was inevitable.

Of course that was further loss to the community which now had no pub to meet in either. A kind of surrender, as Merton would have it. He does concede (perhaps with tongue in cheek) that street violence does have its points:

> It is a way of reminding business, the city, the fuzz, etc., that you are there, that you are tired of being a non-person, that you are not just a passive machine for secreting indefinite amounts of submission.

That reason was a key factor for some in Hyde Park. Other approaches and appeals had been tried, and countless unfulfilled promises had been heard. So far, Merton provided a perceptive and helpful commentary. But as he continues to reflect on the disadvantages of urban uprising, Merton betrays his distance and lack of immediate experience. "The trouble with this approach", he writes, "is":

> It does not make the street any more habitable. (Well, it did—the release of tension was almost tangible. People for weeks gathered on the streets to talk, to discuss, to protest, to meet…and from that time on a range of creative social projects and developments have grown)

> It does not make life on this street any more credible. (Again, not true in our experience. In due course, despite or because of the hysterical media, people were galvanised, organised, articulate, expressive…)

> It does not make anybody happy. (Don't you believe it!)

> It does not change the kind of space the street is.

> It does not change the city's negative idea of itself and of its streets. (In time, Hyde Park began to develop a confidence and sense of identity which had not been evident beforehand.)

> It accepts the idea that the street is a place going someplace else. (No—this was reclamation of the street as 'our street.')

> It accepts the street as a tunnel, the city as a rabbit warren. It takes for granted what business and money and the fuzz and everyone else takes for granted: that the street is an impersonal tube for 'circulation' of traffic, business, and wealth, so that consequently all the real action is someplace else. (Again, not so. They stopped the traffic…)

Merton's reflections might more accurately describe other occasions of urban uprising (I remember the panic in the United States prompted by the verdict of the Rodney King trial…) but some of his conclusions here evidently cannot be taken as the last word. What Merton does provide is a point of reference outside the immediacy of particular urban experiences. And his concluding paragraph is a remarkable echo of some of the feelings which were being expressed during those heady days in Hyde Park:

> They with their gold have turned our lives into rubble. But we with love will set our lives on fire and turn the rubble back into gold. This time the gold will have real worth. It will not be just crap that came out of the earth. It will be the infinite value of human identity flaming up in a heart that is confident in loving. This is the beginning of power. This is the beginning of the transformation. (p.53)

"Confident in loving?" What does it take to learn that? Surely such confidence is inextricably bound up with assurance that one is love-able. And that truth was as significant in Hyde Park as it was for Merton himself. In this essay, Merton returns in imagination to the city, with a heart at last more confident in loving. He had made his own journey down that particular, arduous path. If he had been confident in loving back in 1941 perhaps he would after all have stayed in Harlem rather than arrived at the gatehouse of Gethsemani Abbey. Who knows?

Appendix

In the 'Hyde Park Churches Youth Survey' (published in 1995, shortly before the disturbances), we described the area as:

> complex and diverse, with distinct groups, cultures, outlook and experience. There are numerous small communities, mostly centred around groups of streets. People are very territorial, and there is little sense of a wider community identity. People in the area find it difficult actually to say where they live in any terms that can be recognised by outsiders. The ethnic diversity of the residents and the large shifting population of students also militate against any sense of community identity or common commitment.

This brokenness and lack of identity in the community has not always been the case (some of the recent history as recalled by local people is recorded in Nick Davies' The Dark Heart. Davies has a cavalier approach to fact in some instances, though his analysis is sharp). Loss of many jobs. Around the beginning of the 1990s, the situation in Hyde Park had changed dramatically. The 1991 census records a familiar tale of high unemployment, poor housing and a high crime rate. Many young people were growing up in households where they have no experience of adults who go to work. Prospects for young people leaving school were bleak, and (for example) car-crime figures from August 1994 to January 1995 showed the area to be the worst in the city and burglary figures to be the second highest. We knew young people from the area involved in this criminal activity. Council and other housing was bought up—often by absentee land-lords (locals could not afford it) then rented out at high prices to single parents or students who frequently stayed only a short time and didn't care much for the area.

Notes and References

1. *God in the City*, ed Peter Sedgwick, London: Mowbray, 1995, p.204

2. *Love and Living*, London: Sheldon Press, 1979, pp. 46-53. 'The Street is for Celebration' appeared in *The Mediator* 20 (Summer 1969), pp.2-4.

3. R. Pahl, *Whose City?* London: Penguin, 1975, p.206

4. Ibid., p.10

5. New York: Doubleday, 1969. The author's preface to the novel puts it into context and asserts its continuing significance. The comments quoted are from a private journal first quoted in Michael Mott, *The Seven Mountains of Thomas Merton*, p.513.

6. In the Author's Preface, written in 1968, a few months before his death, Merton writes: *I wanted to enter the Trappists but had not yet managed to make up my mind about doing so. This novel is a kind of sardonic meditation on the world in which I then found myself: my attempt to define its predicament, and my own place in it.*

7. Ibid., pp.33f

8. From *A Man in the Divided Sea*, New York: New Directions, 1946

9. *The Secular Journal of Thomas Merton*. New York: Farrar, Straus and Cudahy, 1959, p.269.

10. *Conjectures of a Guilty Bystander*. New York: Doubleday & Co., 1965. Second ed 1977, Sheldon Press, London, p.74

11. LL, p.49. The first essay in *Love and Living*, namely *Learning to Live*, dovetails with much that is said in 'The Street is for Celebration', not least in discussion of the meaning of real presence.

The Portable Cloister of the Heart:
Emerging New Forms
of the Monastic Impulse

RICH FOURNIER

For we have this treasure in earthen vessels...

BOTH IN THE WORLD ITSELF AND IN THE WORLD OF MONASTICISM, WE LIVE in a *kairos* time; a time pregnant with possibility, a time shot through with uncertainty. The old is passing away, and behold, the new has not yet come. These unsettling times tend to elicit polarized responses. Some people cling desperately to old ways, holding fast to the known rather than facing the unknown. Others meander their way through the ferment and chaos and, seemingly without discernment, become attracted to anything new.

This is a *kairos* time for the monastic Spirit as well. There is an increased interest in all things monastic. Even the advertising world has tried to capitalize on this, with religiously garbed monastic men and women providing the context and contrast to sell computers, communicators and copiers. Books on monasticism and music from monastic liturgies become best-sellers. The question is: is this interest in monasticism a regressive movement towards the past to escape the complexities of the present, or is it an authentic renewal of the charism of the monastic spirit and the lure of the monastic quest to seek God above all else? Are our monasteries capable of responding creatively but faithfully to this seeking, or are they too heavily laden with historical forms that no longer convey the life-giving spirit of monasticism? Have we, as seekers, matured enough to avoid confusing change with transformation? These are questions that Merton also spent a good deal of time pondering, since the initial winds of this change were blowing during his lifetime.

I believe that the Spirit of God is behind this *kairos* time, actively seeking to make people more aware of the "hidden ground of love" and the "hidden wholeness" which connects us all. This mystical reality, or mystical matrix, has been intuitively expressed in Christian doctrine (e.g. the Trinity, Mystical Body of Christ, Communion of Saints, etc) and has been directly apprehended and experienced by mystics throughout the ages. The awareness of this deep interconnectedness provides the foundation for healing the painful divisions within and among people and nature. Karl Rahner predicted that Christians of the 21st century will be mystics, or there won't be Christians at all. The treasures of the monastic tradition can be a great resource and help in this transformation of consciousness and in cultivating awareness of the mystical matrix.

But the treasures of the monastic spirit and tradition are housed in earthen vessels. Merton was aware of this ongoing tension and liked to make the distinction between the living tradition (the treasure) and convention (the earthen vessel). Monasticism is constantly faced with the challenges and struggles to remain authentically alive and faithful to the charism of the monastic spirit. Can the monastic spirit be set free from its historical institutional expressions without being set adrift? Can we find ways to remain rooted in tradition, but not unnecessarily bound by that tradition? The problem of the routinization of spirit is a long-standing one in many traditions. And it starts right in the earliest attempts to pass on the knowledge and experience. As Sam Keen notes:

> "Not one of the founders of the great religions was orthodox. Jesus wasn't a Christian. Gautama wasn't a Buddhist, Mohammed wasn't a Muslim. All were charismatic spiritual seekers, mystics, prophets, troublemakers, critics of the establishments of their day. As Emerson said, speaking about religion, 'In the first generation the men were golden and the goblets were wooden. In the second generation the men were wooden and the goblets were golden.' Charisma is bureaucratized, the spirit is forced to punch a time clock and answer to the authorities. (Keen, *Hymns to an Unknown God*, p.74).

Mutatis mutandis, this is also true for the monastic spirit and its historical forms. The monastic spirit is like the wind mentioned in John 3, that blows where it wills. No fixed form, however solid and sanctioned, can contain it for long. For those who try to capture it, or hold it fast to a particular form or manifestation, the monastic spirit as wind can be experienced as a tornado or hurricane, that radically razes the boxes and houses constructed to contain it. For those more sensitive to its nuances, it can be experienced as the wind to fill the sails of a vessel tacking its way on the journey to God.

The monk needs to be related to the tradition without being controlled by the historically evolved institutional forms of that tradition. She must be rooted in, but not pot-bound by, that tradition, in order to be free to flower in her own unique way as an expression of the monastic seed/spirit. I am not saying that institutional monasticism is bad or obsolete. There will always be those who are able to live a deep, true and authentic life within them. But institutional monasticism can no longer be exclusively normative, no longer have a monopoly over defining who is and who is not a monk. The monastic charism transcends and outgrows any particular form created to contain it or express it. Monastic institutions can become resources and catalysts for people to respond to and embody the monastic impulse that beats in their own hearts. As Lawrence Cunningham points out:

> [Merton's] writings argued for a kind of delicate balance in which a monastic culture with authentically deep foundations could be maintained while permitting a maximum degree of flexibility to allow for human growth and development. (Cunningham, p.127)

There seems to be a redefinition and relocation of the monastic spirit underway—a redefining of what the monastic spirit or monastic impulse essentially is, and who are the carriers of it. There is also a relocation of the monastic spirit away from exclusively identifying it with its historical, institutional, and geographical places, e.g. monasteries, to the portable cloister of one's own heart.

The Monastic Spirit and Impulse

The monastic spirit predates any Christian expression of it, it is an archetypal aspect of being human. This "monastic impulse" (Walter Capps) has been a part of human experience for as long as history has been recorded. Some people have always tended toward solitude, the margins, toward liminality. The monk refuses to settle into the ready-made forms the world provides and requires, and instead sets out on a journey to the unknown, following the siren song of the monastic spirit. The monk is one who lives on the margins of the world to enable engagement with the center of life.

The monastic spirit is present when one takes one's relationship with God with a singular seriousness (not a deadly seriousness, but a lively intensity, a life-giving focus). Like it says over the entrance gate to Gethsemani "God Alone." The word 'monos' itself can mean 'one', or 'alone' or even 'all-one'. It is about integrity and wholeness in body, mind and spirit. The monk is thus the one who seeks to be at one with God, self and others. There is a going *apart* to become *a part* of everything else. The monastic spirit is a withdrawal from that which fragments us in order to promote a oneness within and without. Evagrius Ponticus describes the monk as one who is separated from all and united to all.

The monastic impulse is the "still small voice" of God whispering into our lives that there is more to life than the surface living of it, and that there is more to us than the identities and tasks that our culture gives us. It is the almost silent, but relentless, pitch of an inner homing device that calls us from artifice to authenticity. Or in Augustine's justly famous words, "God has made us for Himself, and our hearts are restless until they find their rest in Him." The monastic impulse is the refusal to rest in anything less than the presence of God.

The monastic spirit needs to be cultivated to be kept vital. It is here that the role and experience of monastic practices can be most beneficial. Monasteries can become resource centers, hubs around which true yet diverse manifestations of the monastic impulse may revolve and evolve. Places where there can be a hollowing out of the false self to make room for the growth of the true self in Christ. People can come and learn tools, make relationships, and have experiences that they can take with them to practice the presence of God in their everyday life.

Monasteries need to be places, not just of formation, but of transformation. They need to be a place where the vow of *conversio morum* is not just a verbal one from the lips, but an existential one from the heart; where the obedience called for is a listening for the continuing call of God for people to be their unique and authentic selves and not for fitting in and being simply a smoothly functioning part of monastic machinery.

Monastic enclosure and monastic observance were not ends in themselves. They were considered a necessary condition for, and matrix out of which would come, contemplative union with God. (Cunningham, p.27)

The essence of monasticism, or the monastic impulse, the 'one thing needful' is to maintain the primacy of *being* over *doing* and *having*. The monk is the one who cultivates and 'rests in' (hesychast) one's own being, which is simple compared with the complexities of having and doing. The sources tell us to sit in your cell and your cell will teach you everything. It is there in the practice of sitting, of contemplation, whether in a physically set apart cell, or a carved out psychic cloister of the heart, that the monk becomes yoked to living and learning the primacy of being and the cultivation of contemplative being and consciousness. The being found in the core of one's heart is the being that is shared with all, related to all.

For *being* is never simply and purely 'being-in-itself'—it is always a *being-with* because of the relational matrix of life. Being is always a 'being-with' because God is the ground of our being, the matrix or womb which "causes to be" (Exodus 3:14), and in whom we live and move and have our being. This being, which is also a 'being-with', has as a constitutive element a *being-for*, which manifests as a desire to transcend self through service to something beyond self. Put simply, by cultivating *being*, the monk increases conscious awareness of *being-with*—being with self (true self), God, and others. With this awareness comes the natural desire *to be for*. There is a way in which one flows into the other, a dialectic of being which deepens both. Attended-to being leads to the realization of being as 'being-with', which in turn opens into a compassionate 'being-for.' So the monk is one who cultivates and rests in the basic 'being-with' and 'being-for' of the true self, our original face, in the cloister of the heart.

Since our selves are socially constructed they are overlaid with an artifice of having and doing. These are not bad in themselves, and are necessary experiences of being human. However, when they become substitutes for true being (e.g. one tries to gain a sense of self worth by having many things, or by doing great things etc.) then one is in need of a *metanoia*, a change, a re-orientation. The treasures of the monastic tradition, particularly the living of a form of the vows, can help with this. St Paul beckons us to <u>not be conformed</u> to this world, but <u>be transformed by the renewal of our hearts.</u> (Romans 12:2)

The Portable Cloister of the Heart

"Monasticism of the heart is the heart of monasticism."
(David Steindl-Rast, *Cistercian Studies* 38)

The heart has always been a central metaphor in the life of the monastic spirit. In a recorded talk to the novices, Merton said that we are called to give our hearts away, but first we must have our hearts in our possession to give. Monastic practice is about possessing our hearts, guarding our hearts, seeking purity of heart in order to make us more truly able and free to give our hearts away in love. Not to give them out of compulsion or duty but out of the fullness of being that spills into a being-for in the mystical matrix. Armand Veilleux writes:

> The goal of monastic life is to get to know oneself—to know one's heart…to go back to the roots, to the core of one's being, where one can ultimately encounter God. Then I realized that the common denominator of the persons that we could call 'monastics' would be the fact that they are all people who, in their search for God, go through the path of their own heart. (*Blessed Simplicity*, p.143)

How then can we keep the monastic spirit alive in our hearts when we are not in a monastery? What are some of the emerging forms of the monastic spirit and impulse that can help us? What treasures from tradition can enrich our hearts today? This paper is really a work in progress, not a finished product. I'd like to broadcast seeds into the wind. I offer a series of thoughts, ideas, predictions and sightings of the emerging new forms and applications of monastic theory and practice.

The effort of translating the traditional monastic vows in forms that communicate today. Here the works of Diarmund O'Murchu and Joan Chittister are important. The traditional vows function to highlight *being* by helping us to detach from the lust of Having (vow of poverty) and the compulsion of Doing (withdrawal). Vows can be understood not so much as static states of perfection e.g. vow of chastity, of poverty etc.; but vows *for* and *towards*. Vows toward the world might include—poverty, simplicity, right livelihood, ecological humility. Vows toward others—chastity, non-dominative relationships, partnerships and mutuality. Vows toward self—obedience, authenticity, integrity, conversion of manners. All are encompassed by and embedded in the vows toward faithfulness to God.

• Vow for Poverty can be understood as a resource to not fall prey to the consumer culture, to hold our lives and possessions as gift, and learn to be good stewards of what we have.

• Vow for Chastity can be understood as not using our relationships with others for our own gratification. This has applications far beyond the merely sexual.

• Vow for Obedience can also be understood as the ongoing listening to the call of God within the heart and responding faithfully to that call.

• Monasticism is becoming less geographically fixed and more mobile. Stability can be understood more in terms of faithfulness to practice than location.

• Withdrawal from the world will be understood less physically and more in terms of getting out from under the formative power of the cultural norms and values, and renouncing the external and internal patterns that keep us separate from God and one another. Sometimes this withdrawal will need to be physical, at other times through the cultivation of alternative consciousness and practices that remind us of who we really are.

• People following the monastic impulse will be nourished more through relationships with other people, fellow travelers, spiritual mentors rather than through the structures of institutions. Small groups will foster the life and growth of the monastic impulse. Peer groups will play an increasingly significant role in the lives of spiritual seekers.

• The forms of passing on tradition are becoming less formal, more flexible and fluid. Practices are becoming more individualized, and more effort is being made to tailor the resources to fit the needs of the individual rather than fitting the individual to the needs of the institution.

• Silence is becoming a very rare commodity in this world. The practice of silence can help to undermine the relentless chatterings of ego-speak that prop up the false artificial self.

• *Conversio Morum* is a way of understanding and committing to life as continuous growth in spirit. The *process* will be highlighted over the product or results.

Rhythms of withdrawal and return, solitude and community, service and contemplation, inner and outer work, differ among various individuals. Resources to address these rhythms will be less defined and structured in advance, but more likely developed in response to the needs, life stage and life context of the seeker.

• Contemplative prayer, centering prayer, Christian meditation, and sources from other religious and spiritual traditions—people are hungry for experiential resources that invite them into the cloister of the heart where the presence of God and the reality of the mystical matrix await. It's crucial for monasteries and other custodians of contemplative practice and wisdom to make these more available for people to access.

• Growing theory and practice of nonviolence in heart and action.

• Teaching and disseminating the practice of Lectio Divina. The practice of sacred reading can help people to engage scripture and other scared texts in a transformative way. People not only ask questions of the text, but allow the text to question them and their lives. This may be done in groups as well as individually.

Thomas Merton himself embodied the paradoxical tension of the monastic spirit lived through inherited forms. He was both fed and fed-up with these forms. He was a catalyst for reform and renewal and at the same time called for a return to the sources and wellsprings of monasticism. People will continue to find his writings and life a rich resource for their own unique dance into the mystical matrix and presence of God.

> For now I am a grown-up monk and have no time for anything but the essentials. The only essential is not an idea or an ideal; it is God Himself, who cannot be found by weighing the present against the future or the past but only by sinking into the heart of the present as it is. (*Sign of Jonas*, quoted in Forest, p.106)

May the treasure of the monastic spirit be carried on faithfully and lovingly in the portable cloister of our own hearts.

Self-experience in Thomas Merton and C.G. Jung: Apophatic and Kataphatic Traditions in the 20th Century

DAVID HENDERSON

THOMAS MERTON (1915-1968) AND C.G. JUNG (1875-1961) WERE two of the most popular writers of the twentieth century. Their books sell around the world in many languages. Academics research their lives and ideas. People attend conferences, workshops, retreats and courses which draw inspiration from their work. There are websites dedicated to disseminating information about them and marketing the proliferating Merton and Jung spin-offs.

They both published bestselling autobiographies about which they were deeply ambivalent. Merton wrote his at about age 30 and Jung's was published just after his death. They both addressed, in a self-conscious manner, the dilemmas of modern man and mass man. They reflected on Christianity, eastern religions, Native American spirituality, war, evil, symbolism, myth, consciousness, meditation and solitude. They were both conflicted about their power as leaders, teachers and public figures.

I don't know whether Jung knew of Merton. It is perhaps not too fanciful to imagine that Jung had at least heard of The Seven Storey Mountain, but there were no books by Merton in Jung's library and there is no citation of Merton in the index to Jung's collected works. Merton certainly read Jung. It is hard to know whether Jung had much influence on Merton. However, in my reading I haven't come across anything that would indicate to me that Jung really touched Merton's mind in the same way as Camus, Bonhoeffer or Fromm. There have been a number of books, papers and dissertations that use

Jungian concepts to look at Merton. No one has, as far as I know, used Merton's ideas to analyse Jung.

Interesting questions are generated by putting these two next to each other. For example: what is it about the narratives of their lives and the themes in their writings that have contributed to their popularity? Do they capture in uniquely accessible ways the dilemmas of late modernity? Does this appeal, which is meaningful for the middle of the 20th century, contain anything prophetic or durable? Do they represent the last gasp of modernism or a new beginning? Obviously we can't answer these questions today, but they form part of the background for this paper.

The historian Eric Hobsbawn has observed,

> The destruction of the past, or rather of the social mechanisms that link one's contemporary experience to that of earlier generations, is one of the most characteristic and eerie phenomena of the late twentieth century. Most young men and women at the century's end grow up in a sort of permanent present lacking any organic relation to the public past of the times they live in.[1]

I feel that one element of Merton's and Jung's appeal is that they grappled with this type of lack of orientation in time. Merton linked his experience with the desert fathers, and Jung felt that he found confirmation of his ideas in the work of the alchemists.

They attract many who are in search of self or uncertain about their own self-worth. Their life stories have been made into ideal patterns. Merton's journey from an expatriate childhood in southern France to his foreigner's death in Bangkok, and Jung's journey from lonely parson's son to world famous recluse are presented as narratives through which we can read the meaning of our own lives. We are drawn by their insistence that meaning is found through the self.

Even so, there are striking differences between them in their use of the notion of the self. One way to understand their difference is to see Merton as representing the apophatic tradition and Jung the kataphatic tradition. In this paper I will suggest a few of the ways in which they characterise these traditions.

The terms, *apophasis* and *kataphasis*, were used by Aristotle to describe categorical propositions as either affirmation or denial, saying or unsaying. *Apophasis* refers to the negation and *kataphasis* to the affirmation. The concept of *apophasis* was given its radical transcendence by Plotinus and introduced into Christianity by Dionysius the Areopagite. The apophatic tradition in western Europe continued with Erigena, Eckhart, the anonymous author of the Cloud of Unknowing and John of the Cross. In the 20th century this tradition appears in continental philosophers such as Heidegger, Bataille and Derrida and in aspects of psychoanalysis. Apophasis can be seen as a type of theology, an epistemology, a mode discourse, a mystical practice, a quality of experience or as a hermeneutic. The western Christian tradition is overwhelmingly kataphatic and the apophatic has been alternatively denigrated or idealised.

The difference between apophatic and kataphatic language, experience and sensibility comes across graphically in the following testimonies by the two men. Among the volumes of Merton's writings on contemplation, this is one of the few relatively undisguised descriptions of his own way. It is from a letter written to the Sufi scholar, Abdul Aziz, in 1966.

> Now you ask about my method of meditation. Strictly speaking, I have a very simple way of prayer. It is centred entirely on attention to the presence of God and His will and his love. That is to say that it is centered on faith by which alone we can know the presence of God. One might say this gives my meditation the character described by the Prophet as " being before God as if you saw Him." Yet it does not mean imagining anything or conceiving a precise image of God, for in my mind this would be a kind of idolatry. On the contrary, it is a matter of adoring Him as invisible and infinitely beyond our comprehension, and realizing Him as all. My prayer tends very much to what you call fana (annihilation, kenosis). There is in my heart this great thirst to recognize totally the nothingness of all that is not God. My prayer is then a kind of praise rising up out of the center of Nothing and Silence. If I am still present 'myself' this I recognize as an obstacle [about which I can do nothing unless He Himself removes the obstacle]. If He wills He can then make the Nothingness into a total clarity. If He does not will, then the Nothingness seems itself to be an object and remains an obstacle. Such is my ordinary way of prayer, or meditation. It is not 'thinking about' anything, but a direct seeking of the Face of the Invisible, which cannot be found unless we become lost in Him who is Invisible.[2]

In Memories, Dreams, Reflections Jung wrote,

> It was during Advent of the year 1913 – December 12, to be exact – that I resolved upon the decisive step. I was sitting at my desk once more, thinking over my fears. Then I let myself drop. Suddenly it was as

though the ground literally gave way beneath my feet, and I plunged down into dark depths. I could not fend off a feeling of panic. But then, abruptly, at not too great a depth, I landed in a soft, sticky mass. I felt great relief, although I was apparently in complete darkness. After a while my eyes grew accustomed to the gloom, which was rather like a deep twilight. Before me was the entrance to a dark cave, in which stood a dwarf with a leathery skin, as if he were mummified. I squeezed past him through the narrow entrance and waded knee deep through icy water to the other end of the cave where, on a projecting rock, I saw a glowing red crystal. I grasped the stone, lifted it, and discovered a hollow underneath. At first I could make out nothing, but then I saw that there was running water, In it a corpse floated by, a youth with blond hair and a wound in the head. He was followed by a gigantic black scarab and then by a red, newborn sun, rising up out of the depths of the water.

Dazed by the light, I wanted to replace the stone upon the opening, but then a fluid welled out. It was blood. A thick jet of it leaped up, and I felt nauseated. It seemed to me that the blood continued to spurt for an unendurably long time. At last it ceased, and the vision came to an end.[3]

Part of the appeal of the two men for us is that they both sought authenticity in self-experience. Where Merton relied on emptiness and desirelessness, Jung relied on strong affect and imagery. The roots of Jung's conviction about the importance of inner experience lie in the intensity of his childhood dreams and visions, his experience of spiritualism mediated through his mother's family, and his reading of Kant and Schopenhauer while a student.

Jung considered himself an empiricist and felt that his psychological theories were scientific statements about psyche as it appeared to him in himself, his patients and the world. Jung's theory of the self is complex. The archetype of the self is the god image. The self is both centre and circumference. The psyche, which includes the persona, the ego, anima/animus, the complexes and the shadow, is given order by the self. The archetypal self is outside of space and time and transgresses the boundary of psyche and nonpsyche.

The self is experienced through the individuation process. Murray Stein observes that,

Each of the archetypal images that appear in the developmental sequence from birth to old age – the divine infant, the hero, the puer and puella, the king and queen, the crone and the wise old man – are aspects or expressions of this single archetype. Over the course of development, the self impacts the psyche and creates changes in the individual at all levels: physical, psychological and spiritual.[4]

The self is impersonal. In the context of Jung's theory one speaks about the self rather than my self

> The descent through the layers of psyche from the highest levels of idea and ideal and image through the concreteness of the ego's existence and the body's reality into the chemical and molecular composition of our physical being leads finally to pure energy and back into the realm of ideas, which is the world of nous, of mind, of spirit... Its essence lies beyond the boundaries of the psyche...it extends into regions beyond human experience and knowing.[5]

At first sight this could be taken for an apophatic claim—that the self is beyond human experience and knowing. However, the nous is, as far as I understand the concept, a realm that includes being and non-being and is thus, I would argue, kataphatic. There appears to be a correspondence between Plato's nous and Jung's collective unconscious. It seems to me, however. that Merton is in the tradition of Plotinus, who maintained that the One, which is (so to speak) neither being nor nonbeing, and cannot be represented, overflows and thus produces the nous.

One narrative we are given of Merton's life is that he changed from being a world-hating ascetic to being a life-affirming artist. This is sometimes taken to mean that Merton moved from an apophatic to a kataphatic relationship with reality. For example, David Cooper in his book, *Thomas Merton's Art of Denial: The Evolution of a Radical Humanist*,[6] maintains that over time Merton abandoned a rigid apophatic posture for a more open humanist position. I would argue that Merton, far from relinquishing his apophatic stance, followed it to its logical conclusion, and that his humanism is a natural expression of his apophatic dynamism.

Part of the dynamic of *apophasis* is the simultaneous presence of absolute transcendence and absolute immanence. So while Jung experiences the self as a distant impersonal shaper of life, Merton experiences that "this inner identity is not 'found' as an object, but is the very self that finds." For Jung the self is an *other* with whom I must learn to live; for Merton the self is at once the most intimate personal subjectivity and "ultimate and indestructible." Merton wrote of man's need to "transcend his empirical self and find his true *self* in an emptiness that is completely *awake* because completely free of useless reflection".

While Jung's self displays an elaborate architecture and hierarchy, Merton's self is existential. He contrasts the true self and the false self.

According to Thomas Del Prete, in *Thomas Merton and the Education of the Whole Person*,

> Two of the strongest psychological attributes of the false self are its "fear of death and the need for self-affirmation"... The need for self-affirmation engages the self "in a futile struggle to endow itself with significance." The false self thus acts as its own source of being and fulfilment.[7]

> The "true self" is "the mature personal identity, the creative fruit of an authentic and lucid search, the 'self' that is found after other partial and exterior selves have been discarded as masks...This inner identity is not 'found' as an object, but is the very self that finds"... "learning to be oneself means...discovering in the ground of one's being a 'self' which is ultimate and indestructible."[8]

To sum up: We have looked at a few of the ways in which both Merton and Jung place the experience of the self at the heart of the search for meaning.

The concepts of *apophasis* and *kataphasis* were suggested as tools to make sense of the differences between the writings of the two men. For Jung the highest value and achievement was consciousness. For Merton the true self is grounded in love and fulfilled in joy. It might appear counter-intuitive to associate the way of affirmation, *kataphasis*, with consciousness and the way of negation, *apophasis*, with love, but that seems to be one unexpected conclusion of this reading of their work.

I'll give the last word to our two authors. First Jung,

> My life is a story of the self-realization of the unconscious. Everything in the unconscious seeks outward manifestation, and the personality too desires to evolve out of its unconscious conditions and to experience itself as a whole... In the end the only events in my life worth retelling are those when the imperishable world irrupted into this transitory one. That is why I speak chiefly of inner experiences, amongst which I include my dreams and visions. These form the prima materia of my scientific work. They were the fiery magma out of which the stone that had to be worked was crystallized.[9]

And Merton,

When we know love in our own hearts... at such times of awakening, the turning inside out of all values, the 'newness', the emptiness and the purity of vision that make themselves evident, provide a glimpse of the cosmic dance...we are invited to forget ourselves on purpose, cast our awful solemnity to the winds, and join in the general dance.[10]

Notes and References

1. Hobsbawn, Eric (1994) *Age of Extremes:The Short Twentieth Century: 1914-1991*, London, Little, Brown, p.3
2. Mitchell, Donald W. & James Wiseman, OSB (1999), *The Gethsemani Encounter:A Dialogue on the Spiritual Life by Buddhist and Christian Monastics*, New York, Continuum, pp.60-61
3. Jung, C.G. (1961), *Memories, Dreams, Reflections*, New York, Random House, p.179
4. Stein, Murray, (1998), *Jung's Map of the Soul*, Chicago, Open Court, p. 194
5. Ibid. p.167
6. Cooper, David D. (1989), *Thomas Merton's Art of Denial:The Evolution of a Radical Humanist*, Athens, GA, Univ. of Georgia Press
7. Del Prete, Thomas (1990), *Thomas Merton and the Education of theWhole Person*, Birmingham, AL, Religious Education Press, p.36
8. Ibid. pp.33-34
9. Jung, op. cit., pp.3-4
10.McDonnell, Thomas P. (1974), *A Thomas Merton Reader: Revised Edition*, Garden City, NY, Doubleday, p.428

Thomas Merton
and the Edenic Vision

JOHN NOFFSINGER

I have the good fortune to live in close contact with nature,
how should I not love this world, and love it with passion?
Thomas Merton, from a letter to Mario Falsina, 25 March 1967

We need nothing but open Eyes, to be Ravished like the Cherubims.
Thomas Traherne, First Century, 37

IN AN ESSAY IN Mystics and Zen Masters, THOMAS MERTON OFFERS A SUMMARY of his view of the English tradition of mysticism: "English mysticism," he states,

> is a mysticism of praise, and consequently it tends to take an affirmative view of God's creation and of human existence in the world. It is...a 'paradise spirituality' which recovers in Christ the innocence and joy of the first beginnings and sees the world – the lovely world of moors and wolds, midland forests, rivers and farms – in the light of Paradise, as it first came from the hand of God. (p.152)

While seemingly directed outward as an insightful summation of mystics such as Richard Rolle, Julian of Norwich, Thomas Traherne, and the author of the Cloud of Unknowing, this passage I believe also points us toward Merton's own view of nature. Throughout his writings Merton continually returns to the theme of recovering in nature "the innocence and joy of the first beginnings." We see this Edenic strain in Merton's reflections on nature as well as in rapturous moments of praise in which he describes the world around him with startling immediacy. Today I would like to examine some of Merton's writings in light of his comment on English mysticism and to suggest the pervasiveness of his way of seeing nature "in the light of Paradise, as it first came from the hand of God."

In his first published journal writing, dating from May 2, 1939, Merton alludes approvingly to a passage from St Augustine:

> "The 12th Chapter of Book VII [of *The Confessions*] is magnificent. Evil the deficiency of good. Everything that is, is good, by virtue of its mere existence. Corruptibility implies goodness."

In this early journal entry Merton immediately focuses on the inherent goodness of creation. The fact of existence – of being itself – validates the reality of its own innocent nature, and the potential for corruption only underscores the actuality of this goodness.

Over the next twenty-nine years of his life, Merton repeatedly reaffirms his joy in creation in the context of theological mystery. In *No Man Is an Island*, for example, Merton continues his exploration of the connection between nature and the original, Edenic world:

> All nature is meant to make us think of paradise. Woods, fields, valleys, hills, the rivers and the sea, the clouds traveling across the sky, light and darkness, sun and stars, remind us that the world was first created as a paradise for the first Adam, and that in spite of his sin and ours, it will once again become a paradise when we are all risen from death in the second Adam. Heaven is even now mirrored in created things (pp.115-116).

While creation is a 'mirror' that reflects the light of heaven, Merton's writings imply that we need not wait until "we are all risen from death" to be sensible of nature as paradise, for we can access intimations of heaven through direct experience. But nature not only *reflects* heaven, it also *reveals* heaven; the transparency of the world allows grace to shine through. Merton often discloses moments of ecstatic communion with the splendor of the created world. In a journal entry from 1965, for example, he recounts ambling by a stream until he comes to its source:

> Wonderful clear water pouring strongly out of a cleft in the mossy rock. I drank from it in my cupped hands and suddenly realized it was years, perhaps twenty-five or thirty years, since I had tasted such water: absolutely pure and clear... I looked up at the clear sky and the tops of the leafless trees shining in the sun and it was a moment of angelic lucidity. Said Terce with great joy, overflowing joy, as if the land and woods and spring were all praising God through me. Again their sense of angelic transparency of everything, and of pure, simple and total light (*Dancing in the Water of Life*, p.187).

We witness here Merton's tendency to take a personal experience and realize in it a sense of cosmic connectedness. The taste of water is also the taste of paradise—of clearness, of purity, of simplicity. In *Little Gidding* T. S. Eliot expresses an equivalent sense of presence: "Quick now, here, now, always—/A condition of complete simplicity..." Similarly, for Merton, paradise is here, now—if we only had eyes to see it.

Throughout his journals and other writings, Merton continues to express his preoccupation with Edenic nature. In a burst of intimate confidence in *Conjectures of a Guilty Bystander*, Merton asserts:

> Here is an unspeakable secret: paradise is all around us and we do not understand. It is wide open. The sword is taken away, but we do not know it (p.132).

And in the famous 'Fourth and Walnut' epiphany, Merton tries to define a center that connects us to God, calling it by that untranslatable term *le point vièrge*:

> At the center of our being is a point of nothingness which is untouched by sin and by illusion, a point of pure truth, a point or spark which belongs entirely to God, which is never at our disposal,...which is inaccessible to the fantasies of our own mind or the brutalities of our own will. This little point of nothingness and of *absolute poverty* is the pure glory of God in us. It is so to speak His name written in us, as our poverty, as our invisible light of heaven. It is in everybody, and if we could see it we would see these billions of points of light coming together in the face and glaze of a sun that would make all the darkness and cruelty of life vanish completely... I have no program for this seeing. It is only given. But the gate of heaven is everywhere (pp.157-58).

Merton implies that the problem of our relationship to nature is one of perception—we do not always have eyes to see the reality before us. Our worship of our selves constricts our vision and turns the natural world into what it is not, something evil or corrupt. If we could see nature with our "original" selves – from *le point vièrge*, the pure essence of being that comes from God – we would see things as they truly are and would realize that we are living in paradise but do not know it.

Merton encourages us to respond to the paradise in which we are immersed by celebrating our communion with nature. In *No Man Is an Island*, Merton asserts:

We ought to be alive enough to reality to see beauty all around us. Beauty is simply reality itself, perceived in a special way that gives it a resplendent value of its own... One of the most important – and most neglected – elements in the beginnings of the interior life is the ability to respond to reality, to see the value and the beauty in ordinary things, to come alive to the splendor that is all around us in the creatures of God. We do not see these things because we have withdrawn from them (pp.32-33).

This withdrawal can be expressed in two ways: we become attached to our false selves and thus skew our perceptions or we attach ourselves to the "creatures of God" for their own sake rather than for the sake of God. As he makes clear in *New Seeds of Contemplation*, the problem is not that the world we experience is evil but rather that we have separated ourselves from creation through attachment to our own egos.

"There is no evil in anything created by God," Merton asserts, nor can anything of His become an obstacle to our union with Him. The obstacle is our 'self,' that is to say in the tenacious need to maintain our separate, external, egotistic will. It is when we refer all things to this outward and false 'self' that we alienate ourselves from reality and from God (pp.21-22).

And the reality that we alienate ourselves from is eternal and paradisiacal. Our need is to be liberated from this "false self," and when we do, our vision is transformed. According to Merton, the way to experience nature as Eden is through what in his journals he calls "direct vision" (*Dancing in the Water of Life*, p.336), a purification of consciousness that allows us to penetrate appearances and access reality. Vision, however, implies both a viewer and a thing perceived, and Merton's description of the process of this connection actually involves being absorbed in the landscape until the boundary between self and nature is erased. Merton affirms that division and limitation seem to vanish, and when this occurs "you do not have an experience," he claims, "you become Experience" (*New Seeds*, p.283).

Besides establishing a theological context in which to understand the connection between original self and original world, Merton also expresses his consciousness of paradise in joyously lyrical passages. In other words, he does not simply tell us that nature is Edenic, he shows us as well. Merton frequently conveys this sense of paradise in language that emphasizes simplicity of form and serenity of spirit. In a lovely section from the third volume of the journals, Merton reflects on a quiet September afternoon:

> Engulfed in the simple and lucid actuality which is the afternoon: I mean God's afternoon, this sacramental moment of time when the shadows will get longer and longer, and one small bird sings quietly in the cedars, and one car goes by in the remote distance and the oak leaves move in the wind (p.16).

The pastoral imagery of shadows, birds, and trees intensifies the notion of perfection, and even the sound of a distant car reinforces rather than disturbs the serenity of the sacramental moment. Merton's language harmonizes all elements of the landscape and disengages them altogether from the flow of time. And while Merton conveys here only a single moment, it is also representative of *all* moments, for all time is sacramental and capable of opening us up to the Eden that is eternally present and merely awaiting an excuse to burst forth.

Other instances of this lyrical joy abound. In a journal entry from 1948, for example, Merton states:

> Since [yesterday] was a fast day, we weren't long in the refectory in the evening, got out early and the sun was higher than it usually is in that interval, and I saw the country in a light that we usually do not see. The low-slanting rays picked out the foliage of the trees and highlighted a new wheatfield against the dark curtain of woods on the knobs that were in shadow. It was very beautiful. Deep peace. Sheep on the slopes behind the sheep barn. The new trellises in the novitiate garden leaning and sagging. A cardinal singing suddenly in the walnut tree, and piles of fragrant logs all around the woodshed, waiting to be cut in bad weather. I looked at all this in great tranquility, with my soul and spirit quiet (Entering the Silence, pp.215-16).

Here Merton casts his gaze outward, again using perceptual details to capture a particular moment at a particular time, but he also focuses on the subjective state the scene engenders, a mood of meditation, reflection, and serenity.

In another passage from the same volume of journals, Merton makes even more explicit the connection between vision, landscape, and Eden:

> ...this place was simply wonderful. It was quiet as the Garden of Eden. I sat on the high bank, under young pines, and looked out over this glen. Right under me was a dry creek, with clean pools lying like glass between the shale pavement of the stream, and the shale was as white and crumpled as sea-biscuit. Down in the glen were the songs of marvelous birds. I saw the gold-orange flame of an oriole in a tree...

There was a cardinal whistling somewhere, but the best song was that of two birds that sounded as wonderfully as nightingales, and their song echoed through the wood. I could not tell what they were. I had never heard such birds before. The echo made the place sound more remote and self-contained, more perfectly enclosed, and more like Eden. And I thought—'Nobody ever comes here!' The marvelous quiet! The sweet scent of the woods—the clean stream, the peace, the inviolate solitude! And to think that no one pays any attention to it. It is there and we despise it, and we never taste anything like it with our fuss and our books and our sign-language and our tractors and our broken-down choir (p.329).

Merton once again articulates a personal experience that has resonances for a larger philosophical understanding of the paradisiacal nature of nature. The intimacy of journal writing invites us to enter into the scene through his eyes and his perceptions, and once again the particulars of the landscape – an elemental landscape of streams, pools, rocks, and woods – open a gate into paradise. Tellingly, it is also a place of tranquillity and solitude, where Merton senses the severe contrast between life in nature and life in community.

In another passage from the journals of 1960, Merton reflects on the awakening of life at the beginning of each day:

The first chirps of the waking birds—'le point vièrge [the virgin point]' of the dawn, a moment of awe and inexpressible innocence, when the Father in silence opens their eyes and they speak to Him, wondering if it is time to 'be'? And He tells them 'Yes.' Then they one by one wake and begin to sing. First the catbirds and cardinals and some others I do not recognize. Later, song sparrows, wrens, etc. Last of all doves, crows,... With my hair almost on end and the eyes of the soul wide open I am present, without knowing it at all, in this unspeakable Paradise, and I behold this secret which is there for everyone, free, and no one pays any attention (Turning Toward the World, p.7).

This passage deals explicitly with beginnings—the advent of dawn and the awakening world hold infinite promise of perfection. Each new day carries with it the possibility of re-creating Eden itself, when for the first time God gave permission for all to be.

In yet another glorious and lyrical outburst in a journal entry from 1964, Merton conveys his sense of the onrush of spring:

All the trees are fast beginning to be in leaf and the first green freshness of a new summer is all over the hills. Irreplaceable purity of these few days chosen by God as His sign!... Seeing 'heavenliness'...in the pure, pure, white of the mature dogwood blossoms against the dark

evergreens in the cloudy garden. 'Heavenliness' too of the song of the
unknown bird that is perhaps here only for these days, passing through,
a lovely, deep, simple song. Pure—no pathos, no statement, no desire,
pure heavenly sound. Seized by this 'heavenliness' as if I were a child—
a child mind I have never done anything to deserve to have and which
is my own part in the heavenly spring. Not of this world, or of my
making... Sense that the 'heavenliness' is the real nature of things not
their nature, not en soi, but the fact they are a gift of love, and of freedom
(Dancing in the Water of Life, p.99).

Once again Merton explicitly connects the landscape with a
foretaste of heaven and perfection. He returns insistently to the
purity of the setting, and the sound of the unknown bird resonates
with the music of heaven. And to enter the scene and participate in it
fully, he finds it necessary to recover the innocence of the "child
mind."

Merton concludes the July 1948 journal entry cited earlier with
the following observation:

For me landscape seems to be important for contemplation...anyway, I
have no scruples about loving it (pp.215-16).

Ultimately, of course, what Merton wishes to communicate defies
the constraints of language, but the imagery points us toward an
experience accessible to all. In a letter to Rosemary Radford Ruether,
Merton labels himself "in many ways an anti-ascetic humanist" and
recognizes his need for the created world as a path to perfection. He
comments:

one of the things in monasticism that has always meant most to me is
that monastic life is in closer contact with God's good creation and is in
many ways simpler, saner and more human than life in the supposedly
comfortable, pleasurable world. One of the things I love about my life,
and therefore one of the reasons why I would not change it for
anything, is the fact that I live in the woods and according to a tempo
of sun and moon and season in which it is naturally easy and possible
to walk in God's light, so to speak, in and through his creation. That is
why the narcissist bit in prayer and contemplation is no problem out
here, because in fact I seldom have to fuss with any such thing as
'recollecting myself' and all that rot. All you do is breathe, and look
around (The Hidden Ground of Love, pp.502-03).

In East Coker, T. S. Eliot reminds us that in our beginning is our end,
so I would like to conclude by briefly returning to Merton's essay on
English mysticism with which I began. Of all the authors Merton

discusses in his essay – Richard Rolle, Walter Hilton, and Julian of Norwich among others – it is Thomas Traherne who echoes most strongly Merton's preoccupations with Edenic nature, so it is no coincidence that in his journals and letters Merton refers numerous times to his delight in Traherne's writings. Most of all, I believe, Merton responded to the ecstatic strain in the *Centuries of Meditations*, that strange and wonderful collection. In this work Traherne causes us to consider an issue Merton revisits 300 years later: how to "enjoy the world aright." In a series of cautionary negatives and urgent positives, Traherne exhorts:

> Your Enjoyment of the World is never right, till evry Morning you awake in Heaven: see your self in your fathers Palace: and look upon the Skies, the Earth, and the Air, as Celestial Joys: having such a Reverend Esteem of all, as if you were among the Angels (First Century, 28).

Like Merton, Traherne expresses a theology of affirmation. Heaven is a mode of apprehension, a state of wakefulness in which we become attuned to what is around us and live in harmony with a consciousness of its perfection. In yet another exuberant statement of the recovery of paradise, Traherne conveys an understanding of reality as beauty that once again foreshadows Merton's concerns:

> You never Enjoy the World aright, till you so lov the Beauty of Enjoying it, that you are Covetous and Earnest to Persuade others to enjoy it. And so perfectly hate the Abominable Corruption of Men in Despising it, that you had rather suffer the flames of Hell than willingly be Guilty of their Error.
>
> There is so much Blindness, and Ingratitud, and Damned folly in it. The World is a Mirror of infinit Beauty, yet no Man sees it. It is a Temple of Majesty, yet no Man regards it. It is a Region of Light and Peace, did not Men Disquiet it. It is the Paradice of God. It is more to Man since he is faln, then it was before. It is the Place of Angels, and the Gate of Heaven (First Century, 31).

For Traherne, as for Merton, the world is sanctified as it exists, and the only desanctification lies in our turning away from its riches. To recover original perception is to attain a state of grace.

In the *Second Century* Traherne again meditates on the divine link between self and created world:

> That Violence wherwith somtimes a man doteh upon one Creature, is but a little spark of that lov, even towards all, which lurketh in His Nature. We are made to lov: both to satisfy the Necessity of our Activ

Nature, and to answer the Beauties in evry Creature. By Lov our Souls are married and solderd to the creatures: and it is our Duty like GOD to be united to them all. We must lov them infinitly but in God, and for God: and God in them: namely all His Excellencies Manifested in them. When we dote upon the Perfections and Beauties of som one Creature: we do not lov that too much, but other things too little. Never was any thing in this World loved too much, but many Things hav been loved in a fals Way: and all in too short a Measure (*Second Century*, 66).

In this transcendently beautiful passage, Traherne once again anticipates Merton's theological and existential preoccupations by suggesting that the resolution to the recovery of paradise is love itself. In a passage from *New Seeds of Contemplation*, Merton meditates on the necessity "to enter by love into union with the Life Who dwells and sings within the essence of every creature and in the core of our own souls"(p.25). And when we enter by love into this union, when our souls resonate with this singing, the world blossoms forth in its original radiance.

Works Cited

Eliot, T. S. *Four Quartets*. (San Diego: Harcourt, Brace, Jovanovich), 1971.

Merton, Thomas. *Conjectures of a Guilty Bystander* (New York: Doubleday–Image Books), 1966.

Merton, Thomas. *Dancing in the Water of Life: Peace in the Hermitage* – The Journals of Thomas Merton, Volume 5, ed. Robert E. Daggy (New York: Harper Collins), 1997.

Merton, Thomas. *Entering the Silence. Becoming a Monk and Writer* – The Journals of Thomas Merton, Volume 2, ed. Jonathan Montaldo (San Francisco: HarperSanFrancisco), 1996.

Merton, Thomas. *The Hidden Ground of Love* – The Letters of Thomas Merton on Religious Experience and Social Concerns, ed. William H. Shannon (New York: Farrar, Straus, Giroux), 1985.

Merton, Thomas. *Mystics and Zen Masters* (New York: Noonday), 1967.

Merton, Thomas. *New Seeds of Contemplation* (New York: New Directions), 1961.

Merton, Thomas. *The Road to Joy: Letters to New and Old Friends*, ed. Robert E. Daggy (New York: Farrar, Straus, Giroux), 1989.

Merton, Thomas. *Run to the Mountain: The Story of a Vocation* – The Journals of Thomas Merton, 1939-1941 [Volume 1], ed. Patrick Hart (New York: Harper Collins), 1995.

Merton, Thomas. *A Search for Solitude: Pursuing the Monk's True Life* – The Journals of Thomas Merton, Volume 3, ed. Lawrence S. Cunningham (San Francisco: HarperSanFrancisco), 1996.

Merton, Thomas. *Turning Toward the World: The Pivotal Years* – The Journals of Thomas Merton, Volume 4, ed. Victor A. Kramer (San Francisco: HarperSanFrancisco), 1996.

Traherne, Thomas. *Poems, Centuries, and Three Thanksgivings*, ed. Anne Ridler (London: Oxford University Press), 1966.

Merton's Understanding of the Mystical Doctrine of Saint John of the Cross' Dark Night of the Soul

CRISTÓBAL SERRÁN-PAGÁN Y FUENTES

GENERALLY SPEAKING, ST JOHN OF THE CROSS HAS OFTEN BEEN PORTRAYED by Sanjuanist scholars as a strict ascetic who had a great propensity for mortification. As Helmut A. Hatzfeld noted, St John of the Cross "became famous especially because of his emphasis on the bitter periods in the mystical life, which he calls with an unforgettable symbol, *La noche oscura del alma* (*The Dark Night of the Soul*)."[1]

The rigid asceticism represented by John's doctrinaires is no longer accurate, for it is difficult to reconcile the 'masochistic' interpretation of the *via dolorosa*, which accepts suffering as the only salvable way to God, with the incarnational Christian doctrine of the religion of Jesus in the Gospels as well as with John's life events, his mystical doctrine, and his sublime poetry.

Thomas Merton was an avid reader of John's works and the Carmelite saint never stopped influencing his life. As a matter of fact, a relic of the saint was found among Merton's few possessions after his untimely death in Bangkok in 1968. Merton's commentaries on St John of the Cross are refreshing and emphasize the need to re-evaluate the Sanjuanist mystical doctrine of the "dark night of the soul."

Let me first point to the Sanjuanist influence on Thomas Merton. In my research I discovered that Merton's passionate love for St John of the Cross resulted in mixed feelings. As Peter France put it, "the contradictions in the life of Thomas Merton produced the tensions that enriched his creativity."[2]

Merton purchased the first volume of Allison Peers' English translation of St John of the Cross' *Collected Works* in New York. Merton mentioned it in his best-seller:

> So at great cost I bought the first volume of the *Works* of St John of the Cross and sat in the room on Perry Street and turned over the first pages, underlining places here and there with a pencil. But it turned out that it would take more than that to make me a saint: because these words I underlined, although they amazed and dazzled me with their import, were all too simple for me to understand. They were too naked, too stripped of all duplicity and compromise for my complexity, perverted by many appetites. However, I am glad that I was at least able to recognize them, obscurely, as worthy of the greatest respect.[3]

In an early study (written about 1948), an essay entitled 'Transforming Union in St Bernard and St John of the Cross,' Merton made the following comment on St John of the Cross:

> Perhaps there is no other mystical writer who has ever set such high standards in the spiritual life as St John of the Cross.[4]

In 1950, Merton considered St John of the Cross to be

> one of the greatest as well as the safest mystical theologians God has given to His Church...[5]

In 1951, Merton dedicated a whole book to the study of St John of the Cross, in *The Ascent to* Truth. He tried to integrate the dogmatic theology of Thomism with the Sanjuanist mystical theology, but he felt uneasy with the dry theology of the scholastics. In a letter dated June 20, 1964, Merton claimed that this book

> ...is my wordiest and in some ways emptiest book...it is a book about which I have doubts. I think the material in it may be fairly good, but it is not my kind of book, and in writing it, I was not fully myself."[6]

Merton viewed St John of the Cross as the culmination of the long Christian mystical tradition of the Desert Fathers, Pseudo-Dionysius, and all the other medieval mystics. He wrote:

> Saint John of the Cross is the leader of the 'apophatic' theologians, the teachers of the 'dark' knowledge of God. He completes and fulfills the tradition of the greatest contemplatives among the Greek Fathers— Saint Gregory of Nyssa, who really founded the apophatic school; Evagrius Ponticus, and Saint Maximus. But what is much more important, he avoids all the ambiguities and exaggerations inherent in Patristic mysticism, and he does so by basing his whole doctrine upon the solid foundation of Thomism, which he acquired at the University of Salamanca.[7]

In 1952, Merton wrote in *Saints for Now* that St John of the Cross is

> the most accessible of the saints, that is only another way of saying that
> he is my favorite saint—together with three others who also seem
> to me most approachable: St Benedict, St Bernard, and St Francis of
> Assisi.[8]

In the same year, Merton paid homage to St John of the Cross by
calling him

> the patron of contemplatives in the strict sense, and of their spiritual
> directors, not of contemplatives in the juridical sense.[9]

Merton acknowledged that not all monks are contemplatives in
the strict sense for only a few have received God's mystical graces.
Merton welcomed St John of the Cross' definition of contemplation
found in the *Dark Night* I, 10.6. when he said:

> For contemplation is nothing else than a secret and loving inflow of
> God, which if not hampered, fires the soul in the spirit of love.[10]

In 1953, Merton wrote:

> ...But those who have made the acquaintance of St John of the Cross
> will find that practically everything that is said about contemplative
> prayer follows from lines laid down by the Spanish Carmelite.[11]

Merton made no claim to be either 'revolutionary' or 'original.'
Merton saw his work in conformity with the Catholic mystical
tradition where Saint John of the Cross stands as the 'Mystical
Doctor' of the Church.

Around the same year, Merton dedicated two more essays to the
Carmelite saint in *Disputed Questions*, warning the reader that in order
to understand the "sanctity and Doctrine of St John of the Cross"
we must place his life and writings under the light of the biblical
tradition and that of the central mystery of the cross. He said:

> In this way, we will be preserved from the danger of giving the
> writings of the Carmelite Doctor a kind of stoical bias which makes his
> austerity seem pointlessly inhuman, and which, instead of opening
> our hearts to divine grace, closes them in upon themselves in fanatical
> rigidity.[12]

In 1964, Merton, in a letter to a priest, told him that in the past he
has been "much more inclined to that kind of 'contemplation' which
looks into the ground of one's being, the Rhenish tradition, John of
the Cross, etc." And he made the following assertion:

My personal vocation tends to be solitary and reflective, but one learns over a period of years to go beyond the limits of a narrow and subjective absorption in one's own 'interiority.'[13]

In 1965, Merton wrote:

...it is in this tradition itself – in St Thomas, St John of the Cross, the Greek and Latin Fathers – that I find the strongest warrant for this immediate and direct access to God in everyday Christian life, which is to be regarded not merely as a moral preparation for a heavenly existence but, as St Thomas said, the very beginning of eternal life, incohatio vitae aeterna.[14]

In 1968, Merton went even further in his definition of "dark" contemplation when he said that

contemplation is not a deepening of experience only, but a radical change in one's way of being and living, and the essence of this change is precisely a liberation from dependence on external means to external ends.[15]

Now we need to trace what Merton had to say about St John of the Cross' mystical doctrine of "the dark night of the soul." Merton wrote at the end of his life that John is regarded as

a life-denying and world-hating ascetic when in reality his mysticism superabounds in love, vitality, and joy.[16]

For some readers, the "dark night" means turning away from all created and sensible things at the expense of excluding fraternal union and our love for the world. For Thomas Merton, "this is bad theology and bad asceticism."[17]

Merton suggested that the real purpose of St John of the Cross' ascetic work is to empty the soul of all that is not God, to clear it of all images and of all attachments to the things of the world

so that it may be clean and pure to receive the obscure light of God's own presence. The soul must be stripped of all its selfish desires for natural satisfactions.[18]

John's mystical theology has, therefore, a twofold "dialectical" movement: that of letting go of all the egotistical desires (kenosis) and that of letting God be God in us (pleroma). The former path is known as the apophatic way (or the via negativa), by which one affirms by way of negation and by radically detaching from all that obstructs the human soul to reach the Divine so the soul is totally naked before God in faith. John's notion of la Nada is the equivalent of what mystical theologians called kenosis, or self-negation in Christ. The latter path is the cataphatic way (or the *via positiva*), by which one affirms God's attributes after one has gained direct knowledge from a living encounter with the Divine. John's notion of *el Todo* is the equivalent of what mystical theologians called *pleroma*, or self-affirmation in Christ. By God's grace the human soul is divinized.

Merton summarized in a nutshell his mystical theology in the following passage:

> One of the greatest paradoxes of the mystical life is this: that a man cannot enter into the deepest center of himself and pass through that center into God, unless he is able to pass entirely out of himself and empty himself and give himself to other people in the purity of a selfless love.[19]

Merton identified the Sanjuanist "dark night of the soul" with such expressions as "poverty of spirit" and "dark, pure and naked faith." The Spanish Carmelite, referring to this contemplative purgation, wrote in the *Dark Night* II, 4.1.2.:

> Poor, abandoned, unsupported by any of the apprehensions of my soul...left to darkness in pure faith, which is a dark night for these natural faculties, and with my will touched only by sorrows, afflictions, and longings of love of God, I went out from myself. That is, I departed from my low manner of understanding, and my feeble way of loving, and my poor and limited method of finding satisfaction in God...This was great happiness, a sheer grace for me, because through the annihilation and calming of my faculties, passions, appetites, and affections, by which my experience and satisfaction in God were base, I went out from my human operation and way of acting to God's operation and way of acting. [20]

John's ascetico-mysticism placed the symbol of the "dark night" in the context of the mystery of the cross where the old self dies as a sign of death to the egotistical desires and the new self is reborn in Christ as a sign of life and resurrection in this life. Thomas Merton argued that

> The purpose of the dark night, as St John of the Cross shows, is not simply to punish and afflict the heart of man, but to liberate, to purify and to enlighten in perfect love. The way that leads through dread goes not to despair but to perfect joy, not to hell but to heaven.[21]

Merton clearly understood that the symbol of the "dark night" can be interpreted in different ways. Merton made the following observation:

Just as Saint Gregory of Nyssa takes Moses through three stages in his ascent to God, so Saint John of the Cross divides his night into three [See *Ascent*, I, 2.5. Peers tr., vol. 1, pp. 20-21, 66-69]:

> These three parts of the night are all one night; but like night itself, it has three parts. For the first part, which is that of the sense, is comparable to the beginning of night, the point at which things begin to fade from sight. And the second part, which is faith, is comparable to midnight, which is total darkness. And the third part is like the close of the night: which is God, the part which is near to the light of the day.[22]

Ultimately, the "dark night" of St John of the Cross is the moment in which the human soul meets God at the deepest center of the soul. The goal of the mystical union is achieved when the human soul is fully transformed in God. This is the highest degree of perfection that one can reach in this life. The image of the activity of fire that has penetrated the wood, transformed it so inwardly that now "...it is not merely united to this fire but produces within it a living flame."[23] The divine fire thereby does not consume the human soul for it "...never kill[s] unless to give life, never wounds unless to heal."[24]

For John, the transformative effect of the divine fire in the whole person

> ...does not consume and destroy the soul in which it so burns. And it does not afflict it; rather, commensurate with the strength of the love, it divinizes and delights it, burning gently within it.[25]

The fully matured Christian abides and lives in the glory of God forever. Merton put it this way:

> To admit, with St John of the Cross, that we encounter God in the "inmost center" (or "ground") of our own being is not to deny His personality but to affirm it more forcefully than ever, for He is also, precisely, the cause of our own personality and it is in response to His love that our freedom truly develops to personal maturity... In the personal mystical experience of St John of the Cross, God was known as "unknown," and the All was attained as "Nothingness" (*Nada*)... Only those with a certain experience of the life of faith are able to apprehend these paradoxical statements without misinterpreting them as "atheism" or "pantheism."[26]

Merton saw that the Sanjuanist ascetico-mystical doctrine aimed at "an ideal balance of the human and the divine." He said:

> Just as we can never separate asceticism from mysticism, so in St John of the Cross we find darkness and light, suffering and joy, sacrifice and love united together so closely that they seem at times to be identified.

It is not so much that we come through darkness to light, as that the darkness itself is light... Hence the essential simplicity of his teaching: enter into the night and you will be enlightened. 'Night' means the 'darkening' of all our natural desires, our natural understanding, our human way of loving; but this darkening brings with it an enlightenment... The 'darkness' which St John teaches is not a pure negation. Rather it is the removal and extinguishing of a lesser light in order that pure light may shine in its place.[27]

For Merton, the Sanjuanist apophatic mysticism of the "dark night" does not end in nihilism but rather ends with John's mysticism of love. The Sanjuanist mystical doctrine of the "dark night of the soul" does not imply a pure negation but rather the highest expression of light, love and truth. God is encountered in the "dark night" because there is no-thing to see. God is not an object. God is beyond any concept or vision whatsoever. Paradoxically speaking, mystics often describe their experimental and sapiential knowledge of God as a mystical vision, a vision of God. As Merton put it,

The mystical night is not a mere night, absence of light. It is a night which is sanctified by the presence of an invisible light... The night of faith has brought us into contact with the Object of all faith, not as an object but as a Person Who is the center and life of our own being, at once His own transcendent Self and the immanent source of our own identity and life.[28]

We are able perhaps to understand why the late Merton still adores St John of the Cross, and comes back to the Carmelite saint time after time, but "now in light of a mature knowledge", as he questions:

If I would now go to Spain and *see* those stones for instance at Segovia
And *see* those spaces (Castilla la-viega).
Drink some of that wine feel some of that sun, some of that wind
Its true raw bite in the spring
And there read John of the Cross over again
All in Spanish... Or would the same old wheel keep turning? [29]

Notes and References

1. Helmut A. Hatzfeld, *Santa Teresa de Ávila* (New York: Twayne Publishers, Inc., 1969), pp. 141-142. Popularly speaking, the Sanjuanist "dark night" is often linked to any kind of suffering. Bob Hohler wrote in *The Boston Globe* an article dated May 1, 1999, entitled "Jackson prays with US soldiers held in Belgrade. Seeks an end to 'dark night.'" The first sentence stated: "They prayed for

morning to come after their 'long, dark night' of captivity." Was Mr Hohler thinking of John's captivity in Toledo?

2. Peter France, *Hermits:The Insights of Solitude* (New York: St. Martin's Press, 1996), p. 190.

3. Thomas Merton, *The Seven Storey Mountain* (New York: Harcourt Brace Jovanovich, 1978), pp. 238-239. Later, Merton got the Spanish works of St John of the Cross edited by Fr. Silverio de Santa Teresa which he often consulted when the English translation was not sufficiently clear or the mystical doctrine required a deeper understanding in its native language. On March 20, 1947, he wrote that he began to read the practical counsels of St John of the Cross as a preparation for his "profession" (*The Sign of Jonas*, 40).

4. Thomas Merton, *On Saint Bernard* (Kalamazoo, Michigan: Cistercian Publications, 1980), p.189.

5. Thomas Merton, *What is Contemplation?* (Springfield, Illinois:Templegate Publishers, 1981), p.55.

6. Thomas Merton, *A Vow of Conversation* (New York: Farrar-Straus-Giroux, 1988), p.56.

7. Thomas Merton, *The Ascent to Truth* (New York: A Harvest Book, 1981), 17. At the end of the book, Merton cited a short biography of the Carmelite saint stating the following: *Saint John of the Cross has never been a very popular saint, outside his native Spain. His doctrine is considered 'difficult,' and he demands of others the same uncompromising austerity which he practiced in his own life. Nevertheless, a close study of his doctrine...should prove that Saint John of the Cross had all the balance and prudence and 'discretion' which mark the highest sanctity. He is not a fanatic... In actual practice, Saint John of the Cross was relentlessly opposed to the formalism and inhumanity of those whom he compared to 'spiritual black-smiths,' violently hammering the souls of their victims to make them fit some conventional model of ascetic perfection* (pp.330-331).

8. Thomas McDonnell, *A Thomas Merton Reader* (London: Lamp Press, 1989), p.291. Merton also called St John of the Cross "one of the greatest and most hidden of the saints, that of all saints he is perhaps the greatest poet as well as the greatest contemplative, and that in his humility he was also most human..." (293). In a letter dated February 9, 1952, to Dom Jean-Baptiste Porion, Merton wrote: "I am happy with St John of the Cross among the rocks" (*The School of Charity*, 33). In a letter to Sister M. Madeleva written in 1964 Merton said: "But Julian [of Norwich] is without doubt one of the most wonderful of all Christian voices. She gets greater and greater in my eyes as I grow older and whereas in the old days I used to be crazy about St John of the Cross, I would not exchange him now for Julian if you gave me the world and the Indies and all the Spanish mystics rolled up in one bundle. I think that Julian of Norwich is with Newman the greatest English theologian" (*Seeds of Destruction*, pp.190-191).

9. Thomas McDonnell, *A Thomas Merton Reader*, 293.

10. K. Kavanaugh and O. Rodríguez, *The Collected Works of Saint John of the Cross* (Washington, D.C.: ICS Publications, 1991), p. 382. St John of the Cross' definition goes back to Pseudo-Dionysius when he defined contemplation in the *Mystical Theology* 1.1. as "a ray of darkness." St John of the Cross understands faith as "a dark night" which "it illumines the soul that is in darkness" (*The Ascent of Mount Carmel*, II, 4.6., 159).

11. Thomas Merton, *Seeds of Contemplation* (New York: A Dell Book, 1956), p.10.

12. Thomas Merton, *Disputed Questions* (New York: A Mentor-Omega Book, 1965), p.160.

13. Thomas Merton, *Seeds of Destruction* (New York: The Macmillan Company, 1967), pp. 222-223. Merton further said: "The contemplative life is not, and cannot be, a mere withdrawal, a pure negation, a turning of one's back on the world with its sufferings, its crises, its confusions and its errors" (7). Merton saw clearly the dangers of quietism within the monastic life. His definition of contemplation broadened over the years.

14. Thomas Merton, *Conjectures of a Guilty Bystander* (New York: Doubleday, 1989), p.320.

15. Thomas Merton, *Faith and Violence* (Notre Dame: University of Notre Dame Press, 1968), p.217.

16. Thomas Merton, *Zen and the Birds of Appetite* (New York: A New Directions Book, 1968), p.81.

17. Thomas Merton, *Contemplative Prayer* (New York: Image Books, 1990), p.38.

18. Thomas Merton, *The Literary Essays of Thomas Merton* (New York: A New Directions Book, 1985), p.349.

19. Thomas Merton, *Seeds of Contemplation*, pp.40-41.

20. Kavanaugh & Rodríguez, *The Collected Works*, p.400.

21. Thomas Merton, *The Climate of Monastic Prayer* (Kalamazoo, Michigan: Cistercian Publications, 1969), p.148.

22. Thomas Merton, *The Ascent to Truth*, 52. See Kavanaugh & Rodríguez, p.121.

23. Kavanaugh & Rodríguez, *The Collected Works*, p.639.

24. Kavanaugh & Rodríguez, *The Collected Works*, p.663.

25. Kavanaugh & Rodríguez, *The Collected Works*, p.658.

26. Thomas Merton, *Faith and Violence*, pp.270-271. In *Contemplation in a World of Action* (Boston: Mandala Books, 1980), Merton distinguished the No-thing-ness of the mystic from that of the atheist. He declared that "... As St John of the Cross dared to say in mystical language, the term of the ascent of the mount of contemplation is "Nothing"— *Y en el monte Nada*. But the difference between the apophatic contemplative and the atheist may be purely negative, that of the contemplative is so to speak negatively positive" (pp.172-173).

27. Thomas Merton, *Disputed Questions*, p.163.

28. Thomas Merton, *The New Man* (New York: The Noonday Press, 1993), pp. 247-248. Merton had previously asserted that "Our life of 'watching in the night,' of sharing in the resurrection of Christ, which is the very essence of Christianity, the source of all Christian action and the center of Christian contemplation, receives its most perfect liturgical expression in the Paschal Vigil" (p.238).

29. Sister Thérèse Lentfoehr, *Words and Silence: On the Poetry of Thomas Merton* (New York: A New Directions Book, 1979), p.117. This poem is found in 'The Newsnatch Invention', a notebook that Merton kept holding his latest writings. Merton was attracted to St John of the Cross not only as a mystical theologian and reformer but also as a poet. Merton deeply appreciated John's sublime poetry.

"And when I am lifted up from the earth I shall draw all to myself."

A Homily

Patrick O'Brien

WHEN I MEDITATE THE FACE OF CHRIST LIFTED UP ON THE CROSS ONE image possesses me. It is, perhaps, the first representation of Jesus Christ in Irish art history. And it is difficult to find. To get to it you have to risk sea and weather; and even then there is no guarantee of safe landing. Caher Island lies on the western edge of Clew Bay: next parish, America! The Bay itself is ringed by the mountains of Mayo and Galway, with Croagh Patrick their faceted diamond. According to local legend Patrick founded this island church. It is a small island, perhaps a half-square-mile; an island, which from the distance looks like a whale at rest, maybe the Leviathan that has just coughed out its reluctant prophet! One way or the other there is nothing in the archaeological evidence that the foundation is any later than the 7th century. Around the rude oratory are a series of standing stones where the early monk-sculptors played with the bare image of the cross. Each one decidedly different, some verging towards abstraction: as if they knew that the cross could bear the weight of much examination and elaboration. On some, circles are seen, none of them reaching, yet, that final dominating form of the 'Celtic Cross'. On another two dolphins swim underneath as if frolicking in the tide of blood.

But on the highest cross there is a face of Jesus Christ. On my first visit it was almost invisible, hidden under the lichen of centuries, a millennium and more of winds and rain and the beating of what Seamus Heaney called once "the secular Atlantic". It is hardly a face. The long years have stripped the limestone flesh and what is left might be a skull skeleton. And yet, it seems to contain everything; to draw all into its compassion and pathos. Draw in the landscape of rocks and mountains. Taste the sea on its parched lips. The plaintive call of the seals, the orchestra of seabirds are heard like words of comfort. It rests on a gentian rich hillside. In its delicate lines you trace the courage and daring of those first Irish monks, who humorously named such wild western places 'Diseart', Desert. Here also you feel the force of history. Viking invasions marked the end of Caher as a living space for the monastic community. A little further south is Inishboffin Island where Cromwellian forces drowned members of the Catholic Hierarchy. Nearby is Clare Island where a Spanish Armada ship foundered, and where on one promontory a Martello Tower once awaited a Napoleonic Invasion. There also during the Second World War naval victims were washed ashore and a Canadian Air Force plane crashed killing all the crew. History like a cold wintry storm lashes those shores.

Over the years I have brought visitors to Caher Island. The great Anglican Bishop Richard Hanson, the leading expert on Saint Patrick, came here after he had paid the cost of speaking the hard truth about violence in his own community in Northern Ireland. We both felt the original call to reconciliation issue from that face. On another occasion Thomas Merton's friend Daniel Berrigan spoke of the healing power of this image, its urge to create a world where there are no more strangers, no more enemies. Many of the other people who have come with me to Caher have been artists and writers who all have a deep love for Thomas Merton. Every visit has been in a strange, or not so strange, way a visit to Merton. A visit to the compassionate face of Christ, the pathetic love of a God which draws all things to itself, and which speaks from all things. Our first reading from Jeremiah contains a moment of such insight. That deep within us, deep within the fabric of all life, the divine secret is planted, is at home.* The image of the shamrock as metaphor of the Trinity is no metaphor or simile. The shamrock, the limestone, the sea, the wind are not metaphor but revelation of the Trinity. It is the very heartbeat of Celtic Christianity, a central strand in the Welsh bloodstream of Thomas Merton. He loved the story of the Voyages of St Brendan—the islands visited on that legendary journey include ones in this area. Merton also was fascinated by the 'Ceili De'—that later reform movement which echoes with St John of the Cross and Merton's own writings and commentary on the monastic reform in the twentieth century.

The Caher Island face of Jesus Christ lifts up all into the loving gaze of God. Merton's enduring legacy, his greatest gift, was in lifting his time, with all its contradictions, to that same place. Its wars and violence, its uncertainties and easy certainties; its gospels and acts in the writings of Camus, Pasternak, Milosz, Zukovsky, the Andean range of South American poetry. Merton read the twentieth century with eyes rinsed clean by the Bible, the Desert Fathers, the monastic and mystical traditions of Christianity, Buddhism, Islam, the great spirit of Amerindian thought.

The Sign of Jonas sculpture with Thomas Merton in the belly of its paradox, which graces this Conference, brings me to that Leviathan island in Mayo with the face of Christ deep in its entrails. And in both all is lifted up. And in the surroundings seas "deep calls on deep in the roar of the waters".

* 'Deep within them I will plant my law, writing it on their hearts.'

(Jeremiah, 31:33)

Notes on Contributors

CANON A.M. ALLCHIN is Honorary President of the Thomas Merton Society and a friend and correspondent of Thomas Merton. He is Honorary Professor of Theology at the University of Wales, Bangor.

CHRISTINE M. BOCHEN is Professor of Religious Studies at Nazareth College of Rochester, USA. She edited the fourth volume of Merton's letters, The Courage for Truth, Learning to Love, the sixth volume of his journals, and most recently Thomas Merton: Essential Writings.

LAWRENCE S. CUNNINGHAM is Professor of Theology at the University of Notre Dame in the US. He edited Thomas Merton Spiritual Master, the third volume of Merton's journals, A Search for Solitude, and most recently wrote Thomas Merton and the Monastic Vision.

PATRICK EASTMAN is a parish priest in Tulsa, Oklahoma. He is editor of the spirituality newsletter Monos and a frequent lecturer and writer on spirituality and monasticism.

RICH FOURNIER is the founding director of the Taproot Center, a spiritual life resource and education center in Northampton, MA. He also is currently a Chaplain at Mount Holyoke College. An ordained minister in the UCC for over 20 years, Rich has been a frequent presenter at General Meetings in both the United States and in England.

CRISTÓBAL SERRÁN-PAGÁN Y FUENTES won a Robert Daggy youth scholarship in 1997 and the William H. Shannon Fellowship in 1998. He used Merton as one of the major Sanjuanist commentators in his doctoral thesis on St John of the Cross at Boston University. He now teaches at Coker College, Hartsville, South Carolina.

MONIKA CLARE GHOSH is a hermit living in the depths of the Irish countryside. She was a founding member of the Thomas Merton Society.

GARY P. HALL is a Methodist minister working in Leicester. A TMS committee member, he has completed an M.Phil thesis on Thomas Merton and spoken at Merton conferences both in this country and the USA.

DAVID HENDERSON is a psychotherapist in London. A member of the Association of Independent Psychotherapists, his current research interest is apophasis and individuation (Pseudo-Dionysius and Jung).

JOHN NOFFSINGER teaches English at St Anne's-Belfield School in Charlottesville, Virginia. He has been a contributor to *The Merton Seasonal* and has spoken at General Meetings of the ITMS.

PAT O'BRIEN is a long-standing member of the TMS. A poet and priest, his parish is set on the far west coast of Ireland. His poetry has been published by Daedalus Press in Dublin.

PAUL M. PEARSON is Director and Archivist of the Thomas Merton Center at Bellarmine University in Louisville, Kentucky, USA. He was a founding member of the Thomas Merton Society and for many years served as its secretary before moving to the States.

DAVID SCOTT is Rector of St Lawrence's in Winchester. He is a poet, a founding member of the Thomas Merton Society and poetry editor of *The Merton Journal*.

DANNY SULLIVAN is Director of Education for the Diocese of Oxford. A founding member of the Thomas Merton Society, he served for several years as editor of *The Merton Journal*.

DOMINIC WALKER, OGS is Bishop of Reading. A member of the TMS, he has also contributed to *The Merton Journal*.

DIANA WALLS is a retreat leader and prayer companion. She teaches poetry for Creative Arts Retreats and Warwick University's Open Studies programme.

KIM WOLFE MURRAY is perhaps better known to TMS members as Ajahn Sobhano, his name when living in community as a Theravada Buddhist monk. Under that name he wrote a journal of a pilgrimage through the Balkans, excerpts from which were published in *The Merton Journal*. He now lives and works in Edinburgh.

MICHAEL WOODWARD is a writer and publisher. He edits *The Merton Journal* and also works as a prayer companion within an Ecumenical Retreat Team offering Ignatian based experiences to people in South Wales.

Thomas Merton
a mind awake in the dark

Poetry Supplement

A selection of the poems perfomed
at the Conference Poetry Reading

Pablo Casals Plays to the Wall

What a fine wall, ancient I would say, of a church,
and the large stone flags are alive with the light
that plays on an old man's bald head.
The head of the cello nestles his neck.
I see his back and his poise.
He plays to the wall, this man
who could fill a concert hall twice over.
He plays, then, for the joy of it, there,
where only the angels come, one
by curious one, stirring the air.

DAVID SCOTT

Antigone c.20th Century

In this uniformed century, Creon,
I find my task is subtly other.
Today they bury every soldier
with pomp and glory: all brothers

under the skin of war. Flags draped
and furled. Last posts. Posthumous medals.
Plastic flowers. Eternal flames. Only the raped
and massacred civilians left to rot and smell

under the burning sky. Do not think
though I am obsolete or that you were right,
Creon. When the complicit screens go blank
and the pundits sleep their untroubled nights

I will take my sole way back
where brothers lie in blooded earth.
Uproot where once I planted, unmake
the cosmetic beds and let death

be seen for what it is. Let the stench
choke the secret rooms where councils of war
meet: hang, like silence, over government benches
before votes are cast: be the sour

taste wherever writers, actors, artists
play boys' games with death's toys.
You, smile, Creon, but the gods of my last protest
are dead. They gorged on death and its juices

swallowed them whole. I go with no claim
beyond our common flesh, its mystery,
its urge to live, its awe to name
the earth, to make a small history

of our loves and mercies. To tell the truth
of what we are and what we do to one another.
So, Creon, to these alone I make my oath
and go to uncover the body of my brother.

PATRICK O'BRIEN

Water Out of Sunlight

Only this moment,
Is there
Only this moment, this
One moment,
Only this

Breath? If you,
Breathe softly,
Listen, there is only this moment.
Always, only this,
Here, now.

How rest
In this given, rest, rest in
This moment, only this moment given?
How offer its
Smallness, only

In this,
One moment?
For there is only this
In which to be,
Only this

Moment,
Here now,
One breath in which to rest
Only this moment,
Only this.

DIANA WALLS

Red

Beneath the street light,
What I knew was red, like fire,
Had changed to ash:
All its richness bled to grey.

I fought it,
But no other colour would come;
No hint of pink, or amber or maroon:
Just this stubborn, nothing-hue.

I thought:
The moon will tell the truth,
Won't enfold me in this grey pall.
But above, all light was doused in clouds.

So I walked away
From the bright neon lie
And embraced the dark,
Keeping my red inside.

MICHAEL WOODWARD

MADE AND PRINTED IN WALES BY
GWASG DINEFWR PRESS
LLANDYBIE FOR
THREE PEAKS PRESS
9 CROESONEN ROAD, ABERGAVENNY,
MONMOUTHSHIRE NP7 6AE